HARRY HUDS.......L
(1896-1984) R.I, R.S.M.A

SHIPPING POSTERS
AND GRAPHIC WORKS

Text by
Arthur G. Credland

Hull City Museums
and
Hutton Press Ltd.
1999

KINGSTON UPON
HULL 700
CELEBRATING THE PAST PIONEERING THE FUTURE
www.hull700.co.uk

Published by
Hull City Museums

and the Hutton Press Ltd.
130 Canada Drive, Cherry Burton,
Beverley HU17 7SB

Printed by Burstwick Print & Publicity Services
13a Anlaby Road Hull, HU1 2PJ

ISBN   1 902709 01 2

This volume is dedicated to the memory of Dorothy Thelma Rodmell, who died aged ninety 13 December 1998.

Always an advocate of her husband's work she would have been surprised and delighted to see his poster designs, mostly produced before they had met.

CONTENTS

Page

Foreword 4

Acknowledgements 5

Introduction 7

Harry Hudson Rodmell (1896-1984): His Graphic Work . 12

Chronology 38

Notes 39

Summary List of Commissions 42

Appendix 1: "Getting There as Part of the Holiday" . . . 46

Appendix 2: "A New Humber Trader" 48

Appendix 3: "Modern Artists are not all Mad" 51

Appendix 4: "Working in Line and Wash" 51

Appendix 5: "Sketch from Memory" 53

FOREWORD

An occasion such as this tribute to Harry Rodmell presents enables us to reflect on the ability and dedication of a gifted artist whose prime interest was in the maritime activity that was so prevalent in his lifetime. It is also an opportunity to reflect, through his work, the dominant position we as a nation recently held in the world when we were truly a seafaring nation. The sea was our mainstay in transporting both goods and passengers throughout the world and our naval power commanded international respect.

Harry Rodmell drew inspiration from this marine scene and particularly from shipping activity in and around his home town. His ability to convey with accuracy the many facets of vessels large and small brought him into contact with other fine marine painters of his era. It also brought him to the notice of numerous shipping companies who respected his work and commissioned him to produce paintings of their passenger liners and other vessels. He had a particular talent in the design of shipping posters which during the 1920s and 1930s were much in demand as an advertising medium.

It is with pleasure that I write the foreword of this celebration of Harry Rodmell's work. He was a founder member of a society which continues today as the Royal Society of Marine Artists, a very active society with a membership of leading marine artists who depict both historical and contemporary subjects.

Bert Wright
President, Royal Society of Marine Artists.

ACKNOWLEDGEMENTS

It gives me great pleasure in offering thanks to a number of organisations and individuals whose enthusiastic responses have made the present publication possible. In particular the Hull Maritime Society and Andrew Marr our President, and Mike Fell, Port Manager for Associated British Ports as well as J.A. Good.

The family and friends of Mr and Mrs Rodmell have shown an ongoing interest in my researches and the members of the Royal Society of Marine Artists are well aware of the contribution made by Harry Rodmell to the progress of that organisation. Harry was a founder member, a frequent exhibitor and designed their well-known emblem.

Beverley Coles of the National Railway Museum was most helpful in arranging the loan of Rodmell's only LNER poster and we are pleased to be able to reproduce this item. Further thanks go to Richmond and Rigg for their excellent work in preparing the photographs for reproduction.

Charles Brook of the Hutton Press has shown his customary professionalism in helping us to achieve the best results within a very tight time schedule.

Carole Barley, Joanne Hall and Pauline Greaves of the Museum staff turned my illegible scrawl into a readable typescript and Steve Howard scanned the main text onto disc.

Arthur G. Credland,
Hull Maritime Museum,
March 1999

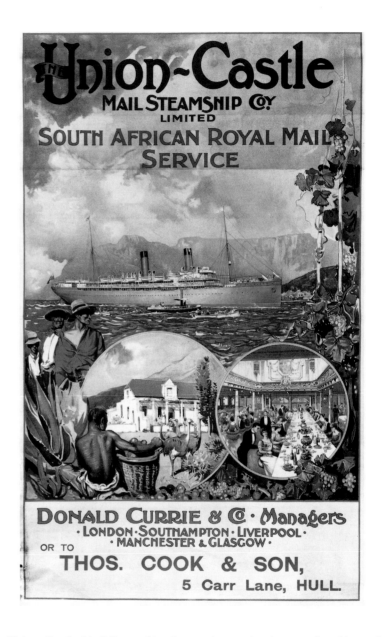

1866; a poster entirely in letterpress; the letters are black, red, blue and yellow, reminiscent of the fairground or theatre, despite advertising the leisurely activity of archery. (F. Lake collection).

c.1910 Union Castle Mail Steamship Co; an impressive image of a ship and explicit images of luxury and the exotic.

INTRODUCTION

Early posters were almost entirely letterpress and closely akin to broadsheets. By the seventeenth century the broadsheet was usually furnished with a woodcut illustration at its head which was either a piece of generalised decoration or directly illustrated what was being described. Similar illustrations began to appear on posters and an announcement for the sailing of a ship might be illustrated with a simple, stylised profile of a sailing ship or steamer as appropriate. It was not until the second half of the nineteenth century, however, that the familiar illustrative poster appeared in which the image dominates and strives to attract the attention of the passer by.

The modern pictorial poster originated in Paris and stems from the work of Jules Cheret who in 1866 began to produce full colour lithographic posters. Lithography enabled a relatively large number of pulls, of more or less complicated design in several colours, to be taken from the lithographic stone without deterioration of the image. For these early examples the artist worked directly on the stone so that the resulting print reproduced his handiwork directly without any intermediary work by the printing staff. In fact the illustrative poster derived from lithographic book illustrations, but borrowed the visual language of folk art such as that familiar in fairground and circus furniture, exhibiting colour to the point of gaudiness and made on a large scale to make the maximum impact.

Some of the most striking poster of the 1890s were those designed by Toulouse Lautrec and he made a major contribution to the art of poster design though producing only thirty-one in total. He was influenced by the Japanese print and his bold distortions and emphatic delineation of the major components of the design were very effective. By using the exaggeration of caricature, simple flat shapes as well as confident decorative lining, in combination with gorgeous colour and bold lettering he made images which made a striking impression on the viewer. There was a poster boom at this period with many exhibitions and the production of special editions for collectors.

In Britain the 'Beggarstaff Brothers' (William Nicholson and James Pryde) exhibited the same large flat areas of colour seen in the work of Lautrec. Their compositions, however, were simpler and with more restrained colour and line produced with a collage and stencil technique rather than lithography and output was small, only ten posters in all. Many artists of considerable fame as painters and illustrators published occasional poster designs. Walter Crane produced designs with simple patterns in flat masses as did Aubrey Beardsley but one of the most famous posters of all time used a design borrowed from a portrait in oils of a child by J. G. Millais R.A. Issued in 1888 to advertise Pears soap it shows a curly haired young boy blowing soap bubbles; it was the artist's grandson, William James, eventually to become an admiral!

Dudley Hardy (1867-1922) was very influential on British design and had himself been inspired by Cheret and Lautrec. His famous Gaiety Girl posters (1893 etc) exhibit lively draughtsmanship and bold outlines against a blank background. Lettering was kept to a minimum and was integral to the design. These are a striking contrast to the reproductions of contemporary paintings frequently used by Pears Soap and Levers (the manufacturers of Sunlight Soap). These latter achieved wide popular acclaim but raised that still debated question as to whether this sort of commercialism was degrading and sullied the purity of art! These two quite different strands in design that of simplification and reduction of an image to bare essentials or the detailed and realistic can both be effective and equally both can fail. If an easel picture is used with little or no modification it does not necessarily have sufficient vigour to 'sell' itself and the product it is attempting to purvey, while abstract designs can be recondite and lacking in humanity and warmth. The best in poster art has originality, freshness and is boldly conceived so as to effectively sell a product or service. It tries to explain or persuade, and is a means of advertising, publicity or downright propaganda.

By the turn of the century, posters were being made to the order of railway and shipping companies. Eminent artists such as Frank Brangwyn were commissioned as well as many lesser names and others who remain totally anonymous. Despite concepts of 'high art' and the dangers of commercialism to its integrity the 'Bubbles' phenomenon probably helped to make poster designs respectable for academicians such as Brangwyn and his composition for the Orient Pacific line in 1900 embodies what became stock images for the shipping poster artist. This seminal production depicted what we may regard as very obvious images, but none the less effective for that, a ship (in this case the **Ophir** at Port Said) accompanied by a gathering of native boatmen in picturesque costumes.

This conjunction of ship and bystanders whether exotic natives, waiting passengers, or idle lookers-on, became part of the standard repertory of the shipping poster.

A travel poster, if it is achieving its purpose, should give a 'build up' of a particular destination and the means of getting there. The impression of quality and luxury (a bit of 'swank'), a touch of the exotic and hint of speed or the comforts made possible by the advance of technology all help to sell the product (i.e. ocean travel) combined with basic practical information in bold, easy-to-read lettering. John Hassal (1868-1948) famous for his 'jolly fisherman' poster, to advertise the delights of Skegness, executed a number of designs for the Orient Line. He was certainly influenced by Hardy, his figures are simplified and strongly outlined but in contrast, they often have curiously naturalistic faces which become a focus of attention. The shipping posters (c.1905) feature individuals in national costumes in a stylised, exotic setting, the light coloured figure standing out against the darker background. Humour, a characteristic feature of much of his other work is absent.

The influence of cubism which became part of the modern movement in art increasingly made itself felt. Russian constructivism and the Bauhaus, the great centre for design in Germany, encouraged the simplification of typography and the development of dynamic bold designs. In Britain, a decisive influence in the progress of poster art was Frank Pick, Managing Director of London Transport. He commissioned Edward Johnston (1872-1944) to redesign the signage and labelling of the entire underground railway system which resulted (in 1916) in a clean new 'sans serif' typeface. At the same time Pick also commissioned a whole series of artists to produce designs for posters to advertise the underground and illustrate the numerous attractions and destinations which could be reached by it. Between 1913 and 1924 no less than 92 artists had been employed in producing this 'gallery of underground art'. E McKnight Kauffer was one of the most avant garde but much more common than his striking abstractions were pictorial and pastoral subjects, essentially realistic, but simplified to varying degrees and executed in strong colours.

During the 1914-18 war the poster became the means of national propaganda and the extent to which the countries involved were aware of its importance as a medium is indicated by the existence of some 20,000 poster images in the collection of the Imperial War Museum.

Railway companies throughout Britain employed artists to advertise the delights of visiting the seaside, idyllic mountains and moorlands and Britain's historic cities. An artist who perhaps achieved the most effective balance between realism and abstraction was Frank Purvis who produced many fine works for the L.N.E.R. He was able to establish an instantly recognisable image for the public at large and not just the 'visually literate', by a process of a simplification and elimination of detail. The large flat areas of colour had the clarity and directness which is the essence of good poster design.

Whatever the subject, or whoever the artist of an L.N.E.R poster it became instantly recognisable with the adoption of a typeface used for all the company's signing which was neat and easy to read. This was Gill Sans a sans serif type which Eric Gill had produced for the Monotype Corporation in 1928, a modified version of that produced by Edward Johnston, his mentor.

It is not known which artists Rodmell admired most but a number of surviving studies indicate an interest in abstract and angular designs. The majority of Rodmell's posters are however in the mainstream of poster design of the inter-war period, essentially realistic with considerable detail and variety of content to encourage the eye to linger and explore. The proportions of the featured vessel and the perspective are exaggerated to a greater or lesser extent, occasionally, as in a Canadian Pacific poster; the large flat areas of colour yield a striking simplicity. He was totally convincing in this mode and it is likely that the predominance of more realistic images is the result of the demands of his clients or the decisions of his agent. The evidence of his own writings indicated that he was not rigid in his views on the forms and expressions of art. Bright modern posters were produced for the French Line (C.G.T.) and the Swedish-American line in the 1930s. A study for a twin-funnel ship sailing between a much simplified mosque and a cathedral intended for the Nederland Line may have been rejected as with various studies for P and O and Orient Lines featuring an anchor as the main focus of the design. There are also a number of strikingly modern studies for Swedish Lloyd which may have been intended as cover designs for brochures.

The inter-war posters for British-based companies are uniformly conventional. But Rodmell's strength was to be able to work within these restrictions and consistently produce images which do make considerable visual impact. The overwhelming majority of his designs are successful in the task of attracting the eye and conveying the message whatever his approach.

Only once was Rodmell called upon illustrate a book, David Bone's **The Lookoutman** (1923) but he provided a number of illustrations for magazines, including some cover designs, especially at the beginning of his career. On at least two occasions he also designed a book jacket and a proof survives for **While the Sea Remaineth** and Jack Harvey's **Beyond the River's Mouth**. In the 1920s and 1930s many famous artists and many who remained obscure or anonymous, demonstrated their skills in this form of 'graphic communication'. Jackets were like posters on a miniature scale, evoking and promoting the contents of the books they covered by striking images, the use of colour and bold lettering. At the beginning of the nineteenth century they were merely wrappers to protect the book from dirt and dust and were discarded after purchase. It was again artists such as Beardsley, Lautrec and Steinlen who first provided original images to decorate such wrappers and showed the way for designers of the twentieth century who made the dust jacket into a minor art form.

Post-war the modern influences had been largely absorbed into the graphic tradition and Rodmell's work is no exception. On the whole we can say of much poster work in the 1950s and 1960s that though technically good the designs so often lack vigour and that extra 'oomph' which draws the attention of the onlooker.

Rodmell worked from his home in Hornsea with occasional forays to gather source material and we do not know how much contact he may have had with other contemporary poster artists. His closest artistic friends were both resident in Hull, Frank Armstrong, the illustrator and topographical artist, and Allanson Hick, architect and marine painter. Whether he had any regular contact with Charles Pears, (illustrator, poster designer and marine artist), before the foundation of the Society of Marine Artists, is also unknown. After the 1939-45 war Rodmell was of course a stalwart of the society but by this time his poster work was almost finished.

Pears, born in Pontefract, Yorkshire, spent time as a pupil at the Scarborough School of Art, whose principal was Arthur Strange, artist and small-boat designer. Also present in Scarborough at the same time was Frank Mason and all three men were enthusiasts for small craft and boating; Strange is now recognised as one of the most influential small-boat designers from the British Isles. Mason (elected to the Staithes Group of Artists in 1901 at their inaugural meeting) was one of the most prolific poster and marine artists of his generation and produced numerous posters for the NER, both for the rail network and the docks (including Hull) which they owned and ran in the north east of England. A series advertising Hull, Middlesbrough and other NER ports has a standard layout with an engraved image of the docks and basic information and statistics directly below; these are referred to in **Advertisers Weekly**; (3 March, 1922 p271).

Scarborough, a popular watering place, was itself a frequent subject for LNER posters. Pears designed at least one poster for the LNER in 1926, featuring Filey, also on the Yorkshire coast, and Rodmell provided them with a poster for Hornsea, his place of residence, published c.1930. Pears also provided forty-four posters for the London Underground from 1913 to 1936.

Mason's personal contact with the Humber was established in 1905 when he joined the Humber Yawl Club, based at Brough Haven just upriver from Hull. Albert Strange was an active member and played a crucial role in the development of the canoe yawl. The members produced a year book which was beautifully illustrated by Mason, Strange and many amateur contributors including George F Holmes (d.1940) a founder member in 1883 and along with Strange a major contributor to small boat design. He was a student along with H H Rodmell at the Hull School of Art and in 1919 both men provided etchings for a folio of prints prepared by the 'engraving and lithography' class, the former a piece entitled Winteringham Haven, the latter one with a wartime theme, 'Ready Aye Ready'.

The outbreak of the Second World War put an end to the production of all shipping posters. Ships and their movements now had a vital strategic importance for the survival of the nation rather than being vehicles to visit exotic places. Those relating to docks and trade and recreation by the seaside all vanished, the only nautical themes now relevant were naval recruitment and the efforts made by the naval and mercantile forces to wage war. Cruising and transatlantic travel were out of the question for the duration and when the war ended shipping companies struggled to rebuild. Sea voyages for the tourist and cruising on the high seas did revive but on a reduced scale and the expansion of the airlines provided an increasingly easy means of long distance travel. Few shipping posters were being produced and this was also the case with posters for the railways. The restrictions created on the railways by the war were followed soon afterwards, in 1948, by the upheaval of nationalisation. The railway station had been a prime site for all kinds of posters and along with travel agents, shipping agents and port passenger terminals provided a showcase for the shipping poster too. Rodmell's own last posters were for Eagle steamers 1953, Associated Humber Lines (jointly run with British Railways) 1959, and Coastlines also in the late 1950s.

Increasingly after 1945 the poster came to be made using a simple photographic image or a montage of images. This approach was not entirely new and had been used pre-war, an example being the Sunlight Soap advertisement 'Preserves My Hands', published 1928-29. It uses a black and white photograph of a middle-aged woman examining her hands, a basket of washing nearby and a pack of soap with its name in prominent letters superimposed. There is a plain one-colour background to the black and white image.

Since the late 1950s the impact of the poster has been increasingly lost. Offices and stations have allowed less and less space for their display and increasingly posters are seen on roadside billboards as fleeting glimpses from a car or bus. The prime medium of advertising is now television and the magazine and colour supplements second.

The period between the two World Wars was undoubtedly the heyday of the full colour illustrated poster. A huge number of artists were employed in creating images to draw the public's attention to advertisements for all kinds of consumer goods, entertainments and the delights of travel by land and sea. The posters of the railway companies and of the London Underground are widely known and many of the artists are virtually household names. On the other hand the shipping poster though well known as a type has not received the same close attention of researchers and exhibition organisers. Few, if any, examples of the genre immediately register as the work of a named artist. In addition, the numbers of shipping posters which survive seem to be considerably less than those of railway and underground posters though they were distributed to shipping company offices, shipping agents, travel agents and appropriate port railway terminals. We might expect staff at any and all of these venues to have collected these colourful and attractive designs and regular travellers to have sought to acquire samples. The relative scarcity of shipping posters as compared with most other types therefore probably indicates that they were produced in far smaller numbers than, for example, their railway equivalent.

One of the greatest exponents of the shipping poster was Harry Hudson Rodmell (1896-1984) who is probably best known to modern collectors as a marine artist, painting in watercolour and on canvas in the post-1945 era. A founder member of the Royal Society of Marine Artists he was active as a marine and topographical artist until the 1970s.

The text which follows is the fruit of research undertaken since the 1984 exhibition of Rodmell's work, which showed a cross-section of his graphic work and marine paintings. It is now possible to give a more detailed description of his career and its development. The author is particularly indebted to the artist's widow for her constant help and interest.

A. G. C.

SOURCES

John Barnicoat **Posters, a Concise History**, London, 1972
Percy V Bradshaw **Art in Advertising**, London, 1925
Heller, Steven and Chwast, Seymour **Jackets Required- an illustrated history of American book jacket design 1920-1950** San Francisco, 1995
D Crippleditch **The John Hassall Lifestyle**, 1979
Edward V Hickey **Kenneth Shoesmith (1890-1939), Paintings and Graphics**, Belfast 1977
John Leather **Albert Strange - Yacht Designer and Artist, 1855-1917**, 1990
J R Lidster **Railway Posters of the Yorkshire Coast**, Scarborough, 1990
David Reynolds **Kenneth Shoesmith and Royal Mail**, Pretoria, 1992
Cyril Sheldon **Poster Advertising**, Leeds, 1927
Walter Shaw Sparrow **Advertising and British Art**, London, 1924
Edward Yardley **The Life and Career of Frank Henry Mason R.B.A, R.I, R.S.M.A. 1875-1965,** Hartlepool, 1996
Norman Wilkinson **A Brush With Life**, London, 1961

*c.1902 Orient Cruises in the **Orontes** and **Ophir**; emphasises the exotic by depicting a North African native in desert oasis. Designed by John Hassall famed for his 'Jolly Fisherman' advertising Skegness.*

*c.1895 Allan Line, featuring s.s. **Victorian**. Large flat areas of colour; the elements of the design simplified and well defined. The two figures are suggestive of luxury and the fashionable.*

HUDSON RODMELL (1896-1984); His Graphic Work

Harry Hudson Rodmell was born on the 28 May 1896, the elder son of Henry Rodmell, butcher of Holderness Road, Hull.[1] He attended Miss Walker's school on the Beverley Road and afterwards the Craven Street school where the idea of a career in art was encouraged by a Mr Canham, one of the staff, as well as by Mr Cooper the art master. He won a scholarship in 1911 to attend the Hull School of Art, Anlaby Road; this later became the Regional College of Art and is now part of the Hull School of Art and Design of the University of Humberside.

From the age of six he had demonstrated artistic gifts and delicate health caused him to spend more time with pencil and paper than might otherwise have been the case. Ships were a constant attraction and he would skip games lessons to take his sketchpad down to the docks. This early love of ships was the foundation of the deep knowledge of all kinds of craft, which was to form the basis of his professional career. Rodmell entered the Hull School of Art in September 1912,[2] from the Craven Street Secondary School, at the age of 16, with a two year scholarship from the local authority.

During his time there he painted a picture of the SS **Eskimo** suitable for a poster which was bought by the owners of the vessel, the Wilson Line of Hull, and was loaned to various hotels as an advertisement for the line.

Though eager to specialise and concentrate on maritime subjects, he evidently took the advice of J.R.G. Exley [3], principal of the School of Art, to study art in all its aspects.   This included developing a range of manual skills including woodcarving; two items he kept throughout his life are a carving of the arms of the City of Hull and the arms of Sir Neel Lorying. The latter, modelled after one of the stall plates in St. George's chapel, Windsor, was one of a series of heraldic plaques which earned him a commendation when exhibited in 1915. A lithographed heraldic design also gained him a Board of Education certificate at the same national competition. In 1914, an illustrated broadside had earned him a national bronze medal at South Kensington. He also learned the technique of etching and a handful of small-scale etchings dated 1919-20 are amongst the material left in his studio.

The cover of a folio entitled **The Echo**, Kingston-upon-Hull Municipal School of Art, remained in his studio at his death. Subtitled **A Folio of Graphic Reproductions**, no. 1, 1914, it originally contained a selection of graphic works executed by various students, the whole being produced by them as an exercise and only for circulation within the school.[4] Only one print (a lithograph of a beached sailing barge) now remains, it is accompanied by a sheet with a list of the contents for issue number 3; and a foreword by the principal. The latter suggested that it might be advisable for Rodmell to become apprenticed to the lithographic artist's trade since he showed an instinct for poster designing. No local firm was willing to employ him without a substantial premium being paid, because at eighteen, the age he would complete his art school training, they would have already lost several years of skilled service and at 21 he would be "out of his time".[5]

At the outbreak of war he volunteered for military service but was rejected on medical grounds. In the meantime, the depletion of employees in the printing trade caused the firm that had refused him an apprenticeship to offer him a job, **without** the payment of a premium.[6] He gladly accepted and the Managing Director "considered him to be the most competent artist with the most comprehensive understanding of what was required that the firm had ever had in his experience".[7] The company appealed for him as an indispensable worker and although he could have gained exemption he continued to apply to join the forces and was finally accepted in September 1918 when the need for men was so acute as to necessitate the call-up of those previously declared unfit. He joined the Royal Engineers as a draughtsman and intended to return to the Hull Art School when demobilised.

Rodmell's first ever design to be published was for the cover of the Craven Street School magazine and appeared in 1912, the year he entered art school where he immediately impressed the head, J.R.G. Exley. As we have recorded opposite a painting of a steamer was purchased by the City's principal shipping company while he was still a student. He also drew a number of designs for the contemporary illustrated magazines.

The earliest seems to have been the cover for the **Penny Pictorial**, 22 September 1917, followed by contributions to the **Bystander**, **War Illustrated** (1918-9) and **Sphere** (1918). In 1919-20, he also contributed to the **Graphic, New Illustrated** and **Illustrated London News**. For the **Hull Daily News** he provided designs for a special Peace issue and painted a watercolour drawing dated 1919, to the design of a local architect, of the war memorial to the men of Bilton (near Hull).

There are a number of small scale etchings from this early period including a view of York Minster and one of the city gates, a general shipping scene entitled "Merchant Navy" and a companion piece "Royal Navy", both dated 1919. Another inscribed "Grand Fleet at Scapa Flow 1918" was executed in 1920. Soon after the war ended he made contact with Ronald Massey, artistic agent, [8] and began to produce an outstanding series of poster designs. Massey had been subeditor to the **Bystander** to which Rodmell had contributed in 1918 and these illustrations had no doubt brought the young artist to his attention.

The earliest printed posters in the Rodmell Archive are dated 1920, one is for the Canadian Pacific O.S. (30 x 20in) featuring the three funnelled steamer **Empress of France.**

This receives a favourable report in the **Advertisers Weekly** (22 October 1920) "When a shipping company decides on poster publicity one may safely presume the artist called in to furnish the picture for reproduction must have limited scope in his work such as the ship and the sea. Shipping company posters are therefore much of a sameness to the inexpert in ships and shipping. It is much to the credit of Harry Hudson Rodmell that his new poster for C.P.O.S. services to Canada retains these distinctive elements but strikes an original note in placing the route along the sky line and the geographical outline of the country from here to there. The colour scheme harmonises happily and the outlines of the magnificent ship are in bold relief midway on the poster. C.A.M."

There is however a study for Lamport and Holt, dated 1919; this is a carefully finished piece in poster colour but no example of a final printed version has been discovered. Another carefully finished study for the same year features a silhouette of a four-funnel liner and the Statue of Liberty. The only wording is ALL'S WELL and it was clearly a celebration of the end of the war. The second poster published in 1920 was for the United American Line; a third was his first piece of work to be commissioned by B and N, the Bergen Steamship Co, which operated regular services into Hull.

1920 (29 November 4 December) saw the Industrial Advertising Exhibition at the White City, in London, a showcase for advertising material, including posters.

The poster which was used to advertise the exhibition itself neatly captured the nature of the display by showing an underground station peopled with such familiar characters as the Michelin man, the Kodak girl, Johnny Walker (of whisky fame), the Souwestered fisherman of Skipper sardines, Mr. Punch and many others.

These figures were all brought to life in a pageant which paraded on the streets on Saturday 27 November prior to the full public opening on the following Monday. There is every likelihood that Rodmell visited this major event and though it is unlikely to have influenced his development in any direct way it might have helped convince him that there were significant career prospects in poster design. The following year (1921) there was a wonderful silhouette design for CPOS, the simple image with large flat areas of colour is very striking and in contrast to the detailed and realistic images most companies seem to have demanded. The Royal Holland Lloyd poster produced in the same year featuring the **Limburgia** is very much in the latter category.

This design was derived from a fine quality watercolour produced in 1920 of the B and N vessel **Jupiter** with fishermen in a small craft in the foreground. Originally in a horizontal format it was probably intended for a calendar but the composition was transformed into a vertical design and the **Limburgia** substituted for the Bergen Line vessel. This is reproduced in **Advertisers Weekly** (20 May, 1921, p.250) but without mentioning the artist's name, only a short caption "An addition to the numerous shipping posters which have shown the possibilities of poster publicity. Designed and executed by Ronald Massey."

A 1921 calendar for Ellerman's Wilson Line is illustrated with two of their steamers. Somewhat later, c. 1938, he designed them a poster advertising summer cruises but Wilson's did not use any artist on a regular basis; though posters survive by such well known artists as Kenneth Shoesmith and Frank Mason.

Posters were produced for B and N and Norddeutscher Lloyd in 1924. The latter celebrates their new vessel SS **Columbus** by contrasting it with Christopher Columbus' **Santa Maria** and a play on the dates, 1924 and 1492. **Advertisers Weekly** (5 December 1924, p.423) rather damns it with faint praise; the writer is somehow unaware of the glow of the rising sun emanating from behind the steamer's bow which contrasts with the surrounding dark tones. A subtle touch is the impression of smoke drifting through the lettering of the main captions.

"From an artistic point of view, the doublecrown [actually double royal] sheet of the Norddeutscher Lloyd Line is most pleasing. In conception and execution, it is meritorious without being brilliant. The theme is one that is distinctly familiar and the treatment is without novelty. Nevertheless, this poster is quite effective and secures a second long glance.

For some reason I cannot quite fathom, the colours chosen for this design are what a modiste would call autumnal. All have been most harmoniously blended,

(Contd. on page 19).

*Finland Line (F.A.A); again featuring the **Ariadne**. Calendar, but year unknown; signed (Offlund and Pettersson, Helsingfors) (16 ¹/₄ in x 9 in).*

Study for a Peninsular and Oriental poster (29 ¹/₂ in x 18 ¹/₂ in).

Study for Ellerman's Wilson poster c. 1935. Not signed (30 in x 18 ¹/₂ in).

Oil painting of Hull trawler Northella, J. Marr and Son, built at Beverley Shipyard, 1958. Signed but not dated (28 in x 36 ¹/₂ in).

The artist in his studio, October 1928.

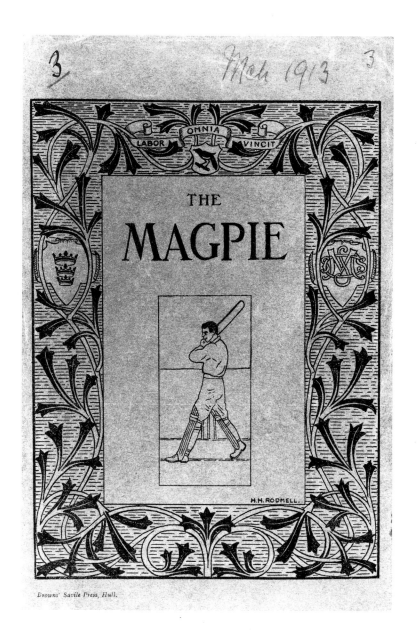

Front cover of **The Magpie**, *school magazine; the design of a cricketer used from 1912-1920 (8 ¹/₂ in x 5 ¹/₂ in).*

"Mines Reported in the Fairway"

"Dawn off the Foreland—the young flood making,
Jumbled and short and steep—
Black in the hollows and bright where it's breaking,
Awkward water to sweep"

—Rudyard Kipling

The Bystander, *26 December, 1917, 'Mines reported in the Fairway'; signed and dated 1917 (11 ³/4 in x 7 ¹/4 in).*

Hull Daily News, *Peace Number; illustrated in colour; signed and dated 1919. (19 ¹/2 in x 12 ¹/4 in).*

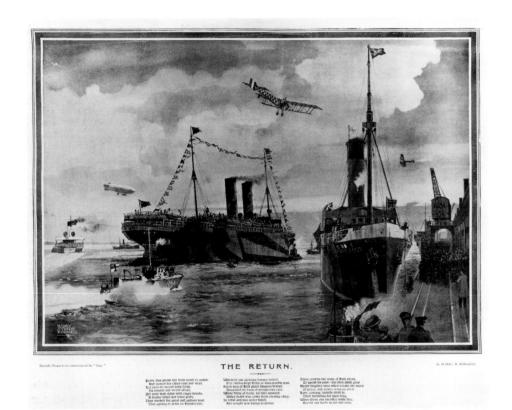

*Monochrome illustration from the **Hull Daily News**, 'The Return'; signed and dated 1919. Depicts Hull Riverside Quay, a troopship, painted in dazzle camouflage and dressed with flags, arriving home; the New Holland ferry visible left. (18 ½ in x 23 ½ in).*

Etching of a merchantman and yacht; signed and dated 1919 (Picture area 5 in x 4 ¼ in).

but the result is a lack of the contrast that is so valuable an aid to quick readability in a poster. It would have been an improvement if either the blue or the green employed had been utilised for the words "Southampton to New York" at the bottom." The artist is Harry Hudson Rodmell and the poster carries the imprint of Ronald Massey 23 Knightrider St. EC4" (reviewed by "Pelican").

Unfortunately, no original study of this survives so we cannot be sure it represents Rodmell's original colour scheme, since Norddeutscher Lloyd exerted a tight control on their publicity designs. In this same year, Rodmell also produced an outstanding oil painting of the **Columbus**, one of the finest ship portraits he ever made, the sea and hull again glowing golden with the rising sun. It is not known to what extent the artist produced ship portraits at this stage of his career but there was certainly still a demand from major shipping companies for impressive boardroom canvasses of their most prestigious vessels.

From this early stage of his career a number of calendars survive, the earliest for Ellerman's Wilson Line in 1921; one for W.H. Muller shipping agents 1923; Belfast Steamship Company, 1924; and the British and Irish Steam Packet Co 1924-5. A long series of tidetables for the tug Company William Watkins of London starts in 1926 and runs until 1950. From 1951 until 1968, the sequence continues for Ship Towage, the successor company, to make it, at forty-three years, Rodmell's longest regular commission. Calendars were also produced for Svenska Ostasiatiska in 1928, 1931, 1934, 1938 and 1939 and for White Star in 1929 and Blue Star in 1931.

In 1923 the **Lookoutman** was published, the text by Capt. David Bone (brother of the artist Muirhead Bone). Illustrated throughout in black and white, and with four colour plates, all by Harry Rodmell, it was an account of the variety of contemporary craft both great and small. Surprisingly this was the only occasion his illustrative skills found their way between hard covers.[9]

The same year a weeklong exhibition was held at the School of Art by former students and Rodmell provided a selection of posters and the originals of the illustrations to Capt. Bone's book. Other artists represented were J. Barrie Robinson, Kathleen Leighton, (posters, metalwork, paintings and costume designs), Mr Foster, Mr Holmes,[10] Miss Jacobs[11] and Mr Brownsworth.

1924 saw the British Empire Exhibition at Wembley and he designed the cover for a Hull City Council brochure for their Civic Fortnight (2-15 July). The coloured vignettes within were the work of that other notable poster and marine artist Frank Mason. Also at the British Empire Exhibition, during July 1924, an "Exhibition of British Advertising Art" was featured in four galleries but it seems primarily to have been a showcase for established names in the poster and advertising field. In 1925 the Empire exhibition continued and a second Civic display appeared at Wembley (7-20 July), for which the brochure design was slightly modified. [12]

Rodmell worked with the students and staff of the Hull College of Art to produce an extensive mural decoration for the exhibition, depicting the trade and commerce of Hull.[13] The Hull Fruit trade panel is illustrated in a pamphlet proclaiming the city's facilities for the handling of fruit; entitled "Hull Civic Fortnight Exhibition, British Empire Exhibition, Wembley, 1925, Hull is the Third Port in the United Kingdom but unquestionably the First Port in Facilities for the fruit trade."[14]

The complete decorative frieze was subsequently installed in the Hull Museum of Transport and Commerce but was not sufficient to fill all the sides of the building and two eight feet square panels were designed by Rodmell to complete the scheme.

Painted in black, blue and gold these were prepared by J. Barrie Robinson from the original studies. One with the legend HUMBER SHIPS AD 1900, AD 700 shows a Humber keel in full sail along with a Viking Longship and the other ANCIENT AND MODERN SHIPS illustrates a contemporary twin funnel liner contrasting with an Elizabethan vessel and a Hull whaler.[15] Rodmell's influence on the activities of the students at the School of Art is also indicated by the poster competition for Hull's Health Week Exhibition 1926. A selection of their work illustrated in the local newspaper shows a very high standard of design. [16]

In 1926 Harry Rodmell gave two prints, showing the railways in 1855, to the Transport Museum in High Street. These were apparently transferred to the special display of railway artefacts shown at Paragon Station and were sadly destroyed in the blitz. Though this is his earliest recorded contact with any branch of the municipal museums there is little doubt that he would have taken a considerable interest in the formation of the Fisheries museum which was opened to the public in 1912 at the time when he was beginning his studies at the Hull School of Art. This new establishment largely the result of the benefaction of Christopher Pickering, a noted trawler owner, rapidly acquired a large collection of ship models and examples of the work of the marine artists active in Hull during the nineteenth century, all of which could not have failed to attract this young ship mad artist.

Rodmell also established firm links with the **Hull Daily Mail** which published two major series of ship drawings as well as a number of one-off designs and short pieces of descriptive writing.

His drawing of the projected new pier and landing stage for the Humber ferries, drawn in 1919, appeared in the newspaper early the next year and a drawing of the 'by pass' (as it was described), or rather 'flyover', intended for the Anlaby road railway crossing is undated.

An account of a voyage in the Hull-Zeebrugge steamer SS **Duke of Clarence** appeared in August 1925 [17] and it was on this voyage he no doubt gathered the notes and sketches for the brochure advertising holidays in Belgium, published in 1926 jointly for the London Midland and Scottish and London and North Eastern Railway companies; it was illustrated by Rodmell and his old friend the cartoonist, Ern Shaw.

The series of pen drawings entitled **Humber Traders**; each with a descriptive text began in the **Hull Daily Mail** in 1925 and continued over a period of five years. One of the drawings, of the SS **Oberon**, was produced as a result of Rodmell's invitation, along with local dignitaries, shipping agents etc. to sail on the vessel's first voyage out of Hull, a journey also recorded by him in the pages of the **Hull Daily Mail**.[18]

Twenty-four original drawings from the **Humber Traders** series were suitably framed and labelled and through the courtesy of the editor of the **Hull Daily Mail** displayed in the museum of Commerce and Transport.[19]

Three articles entitled "By tide and shore on the Humber and its tributaries, changes in forty years in the lives of a silent people" appeared under the by-line "Reminiscences of a roamer" in the **Hull Daily Mail** during January 1926.

Each is accompanied by two sketches also anonymous; the first article has an illustration of sloops, keels and canal boats in a lock pit and a six-masted schooner in full sail; the second shows Hull pier and a sailing ship and steamer in dock and the third a steamer off the pier at night and a waterman sculling.[20] These illustrations, were pasted into Rodmell's collection of proofs and miscellanea confirming them as his work; he did not however include the text which strongly suggests that this was provided by someone else. Some of the cuttings appear on the same sheet with a newspaper extract illustrating the eight feet square panels for the museum described above and are also accompanied by reproductions cut from a brochure advertising the attractions of Scarborough. The latter are the Spa and South Bay, Peasholme Park, North Bay and the Italian Gardens. They are drawn in the same vein as the sketches for the Hull-Zeebrugge brochure and probably also date from 1926 or thereabouts.

All the while he was achieving professional success and making a considerable reputation he never cut himself off from life in the community, such that in 1927 we find him painting the scenery for a children's review by the 'Hornsea Imps'. The original designs were sold in aid of the War Memorial Cottage Hospital.

At this time a variety of publicity work was being produced for the Batavier Line, CPOS, British and Irish, Deutsche Afrika Dienst, Royal Holland Lloyd, Royal Mail, United American, Westcott and Laurance and also W.H. Muller and Wainright Bros. shipping agents. A pen drawing of the **Gripsholm** arriving in Gothenburg was published in **Motorship** in 1925.

The list of shipping companies for which he provided design work continued to increase including the Australia and Commonwealth Line, P and O, Swedish American Line and McBraynes the Scottish ferry and coach operators. A steady stream of work for the Finland Line continued into the 1930s.

In 1926, Rodmell produced the first of the long series of tidetables for William Watkins, tug owners of London, continuous until 1941 but halted at the height of the war and resumed in 1944. After 1950 he continued to design calendars for the successor company until 1968. Calendars survive for the Bergen Steamship Co (B and N) 1948, 1950, 1951 and 1953 and for the Euxine Shipping Co for 1953 and 1955-57.

Fourteen pen and ink drawings illustrating the "Guardships of the Humber" appeared in the **Hull Daily Mail**, 1927-8.[21] A black and white drawing of the **C.A. Larsen** (whale factory ship) was published in the **Geographical Review** in 1929 courtesy of the curator of Hull Museums. Originally published in the **Hull Daily Mail**, April 1927, the drawing had evidently been given to the museum either by the newspaper or directly by the artist.

A photograph published in the **Hull Daily Mail** (26 October 1928) shows the artist seated, pipe in mouth, with studies for two posters in front of him, one for Shaw Savill and Albion and the other for the General Steam Navigation Co, (Southend, Margate and Ramsgate), and an array of jam jars and containers with paints and brushes on a table. The caption reads "photo of Mr. Hy. Rodmell, of Hornsea, taken in his studio. Mr Rodmell is a celebrated poster artist, and has designed posters for the Canadian Railways and leading Steamship companies, and is

*The artist's more mature design for **The Magpie**, school magazine; used from 1920 to 1969. (8 ¹/2 in x 5 ¹/2 in).*

*Original pen drawing of a Hull trawler; one of the illustrations for **The Lookoutman**, 1923, signed HR (Picture area 15 in x 10 ¹/2 in).*

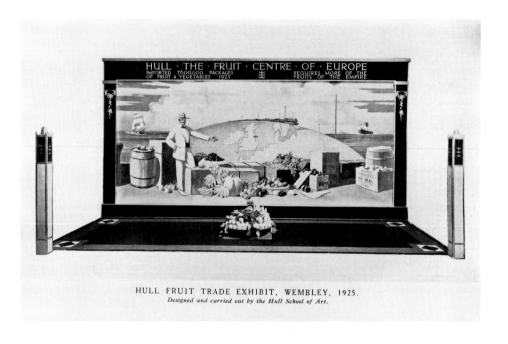

HULL FRUIT TRADE EXHIBIT, WEMBLEY, 1925.
Designed and carried out by the Hull School of Art.

*Cover for the brochure to the Hull Corporation's Civic Fortnight display at the British Empire Exhibition, Wembley, 1924; signed HR. Depicts Wilson line vessel, an old whaleship (derived from model of **Harpooner** in The Hull maritime museum) and Viking longship sporting the city's coat of arms.*

From leaflet for Hull Fruit Trade exhibition, Hull Civic Fortnight, British Empire Exhibition, Wembley, 1925.

considered to be the leading marine artist in this country".

Rodmell was brought up in Hull and lived his adult life in Hornsea.[22] He involved himself closely in various civic projects for Hull, intended to raise the profile of the city in the country at large, supporting the activities of the local maritime museum and encouraging artistic endeavour in the region through his active participation in local art societies and involvement with the Ferens Art Gallery. His pen and brush was always at the disposal of local charities particularly the sailors' orphanage (Sailors Children's Society), R.N.M.D.S.F., R.N.L.I. and of course his old school, Craven Street, which was renamed Malet Lambert High School in 1932.

In the spring of 1929 Norddeutscher Lloyd held an advertising competition and the entries were displayed at an exhibition in Berlin in August that year during an international Advertising Conference. All the eleven prizewinners were either German or Austrian but a design submitted by Rodmell was accepted for publication the following year. [23]

In 1929 again with his old friend Ern Shaw he illustrated **Joy Rays**, a booklet produced by Hull Rotary to raise funds for the Hull Royal Infirmary.

It is remarkable that the exhibition displayed at the Town Docks Museum 24th August to the 23rd September, 1984, was Rodmell's first **one-man** show, not only in the City of Hull but anywhere, and it was sad that it had to be posthumous. He did however share the stage with Ern Shaw 24 when in 1929 he showed at the Hull City Hall a large sample of the posters and publicity material designed for his shipping clients (**Hull Daily Mail**, 30 January 1929) and a brochure with foreword by Percy V Bradshaw (author of 'The Art of the Illustrator', 'Art in Advertising' etc.) was sold in aid of the Victoria Children's Hospital.

The black and white illustrations consisted of a caricature by Ern Shaw of Rodmell and one of Rodmell by Ern Shaw, on the front cover, and inside a full page cartoon by Ern Shaw of 'The Gay Goblins' opposite a reproduction of Rodmell's 1928 Christmas card design. On the inside of the back cover there appeared a delightful caricature of Rodmell in his studio signed and dated Ern Shaw, 1924.[24]

An appreciation of the exhibition by Percy Bradshaw appeared in the **Hull News** and he has the following to say about Rodmell: "He concentrates almost solely on marine subjects-posters for the Shipping Companies, showcards and booklets, etchings and line drawings, showing shipping in all its aspects. He has a remarkable technical range. His decorative pen and ink drawings are always admirable in design and they show great knowledge of historical periods in shipbuilding. He tackles with equal facility the shipping of the past and present, and its small wonder that he has taken his place among the small and exclusive group of marine artists whose work is in a constant request for every purpose of advertisement and book illustration where sea subjects are required."

According to Who's Who In Art (1950) an assemblage of 'Posters and Shipping Publicity' was displayed at Derby, Lincoln, Bath, Bournemouth and on the continent in Paris.[25]

Posters were very much the focus of public attention at this time. The British Society of Poster Designers had staged a touring exhibition in 1927 and the following year there was a major display at Burlington House to celebrate the first twenty years of posters for the London Underground. Here a notice read **There is no catalogue. A good poster speaks for itself**. There were regular exhibitions of posters commissioned by the LNER, that for 1932 is reviewed in the pages of **Commercial Art**.[26] One of Rodmell's designs in the modern idiom was published for the Swedish American Line in 1933,[27] but his typical output was essentially more traditional and realistic.

The shipping companies which continued to provide work between 1935 and the outbreak of war were British India, German Africa Lines (1936), Swedish East Asiatic, HAPAG and the General Steam Navigation Co as well as Coast Lines, Ulster Imperial Lines, British and Irish, Burns and Laird and D.F.D.S. In 1936 colour illustrations were contributed for the contents and the covers of various issues of the **Shipping Wonders of the World**, a work issued in 55 parts and subsequently in two bound volumes. Work was executed for Harland and Wolff and a cover for the **Tyneside Review** in 1939. His covers for **Ashore and Afloat** continued to appear and advertising work was done for Stathers a local wallpaper manufacturer.

He produced a number of lino cuts in the 1930s probably for his own satisfaction rather than for sale. The most effective is a port view of the old sailing warship HM **Nile** signed and dated 1934.

In the years immediately before the Second World War Rodmell had clearly established his reputation as a designer and as a marine artist. This status was formally recognised by his election to the S.G.A. in 1936; a body which also accepted his friend Allanson Hick the Hull architect and marine artist the same year. Rodmell was elected a fellow of the Royal Society of Arts in 1937 and also contributed a painting of the **Mauretania** to the Sea Power Exhibition. The latter occasion was influential in focusing public attention on the marine arts and ultimately forging an association of marine artists. [28]

The majority of Rodmell's shipping posters were published in the inter-war period though only a handful were dated. In 1931 posters, large and small, were produced for Band N and the artists links with this company continued till the late 1950s. Joining that band of eminent designers which included Purvis, Newbould and Mason, he produced a poster in 1930 for the LNER, entitled "Hornsea, Lakeland by the Sea." It advertised the twin delights of his own place of residence, the sea and the lake known as Hornsea Mere, favoured by anglers and small boaters. He produced graphic work for Coastlines from the 1930s through to the l950s, the Blue Star Line, B and I, (throughout the 1930s), Burns and Laird, Nederland Line, Norddeutscher Lloyd (until 1935) and Swedish East Asiatic until 1939.

For the Port of Hull Sailors Children's Society he produced the cover design for their magazine **Ashore and Afloat**, in 1931, the first of three designs used until 1957. He also designed the cover of the Port of Hull Society's mission magazine, **Helmsman**, in 1932 and of the society's history, **Adventure in Sympathy**, 1935.

Cementing his contacts with the Hull Museum, he produced a mural frieze for the Fisheries Museum. Newly decorated, the walls were canary yellow providing a bright and cheerful setting for the outstanding collection of marine paintings, models and other nautical exhibits. [29] His illustrative work appears in a special souvenir edition of the **Shipbuilder and Marine Engineer** (1935) in the form of an artist's impression of the **Normandie** the crack liner newly launched for C.G.T. The previous year he also provided one of his many images of wooden warships of bygone times for the **Help Yourself Annual** published by the Stock Exchange Dramatic and Operatic Society. The publication included stories by Dorothy L Sayers, Herbert Shaw, Douglas Newton, Edmund Small etc with full page drawing by H A Lingham, Charles Robinson R I and comic illustrations by Fred Buchanan, A H Davies, Laurence East and Hynes. Receipts from sales were distributed to charity. [30]

While on business in the north east Rodmell saw the liner **Berengaria** at Jarrow in 1938. Formerly the **Imperator** she was taken as reparation from Germany after the 1914-1918 war and allocated to the Cunard fleet. As he recalled in an interview with a **Hull Daily Mail** reporter forty years later, when he gave a watercolour painting entitled "Berengaria's Last Berth" to the Ferens Art Gallery:- "I was able to make a few rough sketches and take a hasty photograph which I used some years later for the painting". [31]

In 1939 he gave to the Museum of Fisheries and Shipping the oil painting of the **Columbus** painted in 1922 or 1924 for Norddeutscher Lloyd. [32] He regarded it as his best work up till then and had reclaimed it from the shipping company by painting for them in return a picture of the **Bremen**, the most recent addition to the fleet. At the outbreak of war the **Columbus** was scuttled by her German crew to prevent her falling into allied hands and Thomas Sheppard the Curator always alert to ways of publicising the museum, soon transferred the picture to the central museum in Albion street where it could be more readily seen by the general public. [33] Fortunately it must have been returned to the maritime collection before the bombing raid in 1943 which destroyed the Albion street museum, for it still survives intact as an outstanding example of Rodmell's prewar style of painting.

On 22 February 1939, in company with Allanson Hick, [34] he attended what was to be the first meeting of the Society of Marine Artists, in the library of the Royal Cruising Club, at the Welbeck Hotel (London W.I.); thirty-two artists were present with Charles Pears in the chair. [35] Plans were made to stage in due course an exhibition of members' work but the outbreak of hostilities put a stop to that. However, the infant society made an impression at the Royal Academy in the United Artists Exhibition of 1940, in aid of the Lord Mayor's Red Cross and St. John Fund and the Artists General Benevolent Institution. Overall, more than 2000 paintings, watercolours and sculptures were put on display including work by thirty-four acknowledged members of the S.M.A. [36] Harry Rodmell (then living at 6 St Nicholas Mount, Newbegin, Hornsea) [37] showed a 'carbon and wash' piece entitled "**Mauretania's** last Farewell"; an impression of the famous old liner passing Scarborough on her way to the breaker's yard, 2 July 1935. Presumably, this was the piece he had already displayed at the Sea Power Exhibition in 1937.

Hick showed an oil of the "Arrival of the **Archibald Russel**" and a watercolour of "The Torpedoed **Olivegrove**". Rodmell did not exhibit at the second (1942) or third, (1943) United Artists exhibitions but in the latter Hick showed the watercolour "Trawlers Fitting" and "Harvest from the **Heronspool**". [38]

When the Society of Marine Artists began to function again after the war both men contributed to the first exhibition, held at the Guildhall Gallery in November/December 1946. [39] They also served on the council of the society (from 1966 the Royal Society of Marine Artists) Rodmell 1948-1962 and Hick 1947-1962, and were frequently members of the hanging and selection committees. [40]

*Original pen drawing of M.V **Essex** for Humber Traders series but apparently, not published, (Picture area 12 in x 17 ¹/₂ in).*

*Original pen drawing of the s.s. **Highlander** Aberdeen, Newcastle and Hull Steamship Company; signed. Published as number 20, 28 August 1925 in The Humber Traders Series, **Hull Daily Mail** (Picture area 12 in x 17 ¹/₂ in).*

"REPULSE"

"DIDO"

Original pen drawing of HMS **Repulse**, *no. 8 in the Guardships of the Humber Series, 9 November 1928,* **Hull Daily Mail** *(Picture area 12 in x 17 in).*

Original pen drawing of HMS **Dido** with a Humber Keel in the foreground, no. 13 in the Guardships of the Humber series, 14 February 1930, **Hull Daily Mail** (Picture area 12 in x 17 in).

Hick and Rodmell no doubt constantly encouraged one another in their artistic endeavours. One suspects that the rather retiring Rodmell might have been less likely to have taken an active role in the affairs of the R.S.M.A. without his friend's promptings and friendly rivalry. Hick also was a regular contributor to the Royal Academy sending marines there from 1935 to 1949 and topographical subjects in 1950, 1954, and 1955. Rodmell exhibited at the academy only once, in 1949, showing a watercolour of Marrick Priory, Swaledale, and another entitled "Merchantmen". "Tramp of the Seven Seas" had been accepted in 1947 but not hung through lack of space.

He was a member of the local Observer Corps for the duration and an example of a card he designed for Christmas 1941 survives in the Rodmell archive. He also held evening classes in Hornsea for members of the armed forces.

Already before the outbreak of hostilities he had been a teacher at the Hull College of Art from 1931 to 1935, and presumably had given intermittent tuition there even before, since we have already noted his close contact with the students and staff esp. 1925-27. During the 1939-45 war Rodmell exhibited only at the 1940 United Artist Exhibition and it was surprising that he was never called on, as were some of his fellow members of the Society of Marine Artists, either as an official war artist or to provide the subjects for the morale-boosting posters produced by several government agencies. His series of fourteen pen drawings of "Humber Guardships" previously published in the **Hull Daily Mail** were reprinted in the quarterly periodical **Bystander**, starting in October 1940 and ending in April 1942; two subjects each with a full historical description were put in each issue. Evidently he or the newspaper had given the originals to the Hull Museums since they are credited as being published by courtesy of Tom Sheppard, Director of Museums. He lent material for the Merchant Navy Exhibition at the Mortimer Galleries of the Hull City Hall, 8th to 21st February, 1943, which attracted 2700 visitors and raised £100.

A colour cover for the **Trade of Hull and Humber Ports** introduced in 1938 was used until 1946 despite its gothic style lettering and somewhat Teutonic appearance. A new design in 1947 was employed only for that one year.

To help raise funds in aid of the merchant service he and Allanson Hick supplied a display of photographs and pictorial work illustrating the role of the Merchant Navy in wartime which was shown in a shop window in Market Street, Bradford. For another flag day the same year, 1942, he designed a lifeboat emblem for the Sailors Orphan Home, Newland, Hull. Owing to the shortage of steel pins this was made in such a way that a cord was attached to the top which could be slipped through any convenient button-hole!

I can discover no other important works executed during the period of the 1939-45 war, but though jobs may have been in short supply this gave Rodmell time to meet, court and eventually marry Dorothy Thelma Fisher in 1943.[41] Commissions did begin to appear again after the war ended, familiar names such as the Bergen Steamship Co and General Steam Navigation are prominent but the great days of transatlantic liners and ocean cruising were coming to a close. Many companies had suffered severe losses and were trying to rebuild their fleets. Most of the once luxurious transatlantic steamers had been stripped to use as troop ships or otherwise converted and it was a difficult and expensive task to refurbish and re-equip them in the face of post-war shortages. Air travel became a serious alternative for the luxury traveller and increasingly European and Worldwide travel became accessible to a wider public. Rodmell was more than willing to adapt to the changing environment though there were opportunities for producing graphic work for local companies such as Websters (manufacturers of marine paints) and the shipbuilders Cook, Welton and Gemmell of Beverley and Cochranes of Selby.

In 1948 he prepared a series of silhouettes of trawlers built by Cook, Welton and Gemmell between 1883 and 1948. These were reproduced as a chart in the company's publicity brochure which was brought up to date in a later edition with a silhouette of a 1952 trawler. Most of his time was spent teaching, (the Hornsea Evening Institute until 1958; the Hornsea Institute of Further Education from 1958 to 1973) a vigorous involvement in local art groups, and contributions to exhibitions in Hull and the north region. An increasing number of both topographical and ship-related drawings and oils were being sold through these exhibitions or by private commission and there was of course the annual showcase of the Society of Marine Artists in the Guildhall Gallery, and later in Pall Mall.

A drawing or painting might be required before the vessel had been completed and he would work directly from the plans sent by the builders. An example of this approach is a picture of the trawler **Cape Trafalgar** launched in 1958 which he executed for Cook, Welton and Gemmell at the Beverley shipyard. This canvas hung in the office foyer until the yard closed in 1977. In spring 1949 Harry Rodmell also accepted an invitation to paint a picture of the **Port Brisbane** newly commissioned for the Port Line.

He had of course participated in the inaugural exhibition of the Society of Marine Artists at the Guildhall, London, opened on the 14th November 1946 by A.V. Alexander, formerly first Lord of the Admiralty, and at the time Minister of Defence. Earlier that year the Navy Art Exhibition had shown over seventy paintings by SMA members. Also in 1946 his 'The Old Lady - HMS **Warspite**' was hung in the Salon de Marine, Paris.

Only two of Rodmell's overseas clients for poster designs commissioned work after 1945, these were C.G.T. and the Bergen Steamship Co. For the latter he was still producing a wide variety of designs for menus, brochures, leaflets etc and the connection was clearly influenced by the strong links of the company with Hull and the local shipping and travel agents John Good and Sons.

Posters were produced in some numbers for British companies including the Hull based Associated Humber Lines (a joint operation between British Railways and Ellerman's Wilson Line). These were published in 1952, 1955 and finally in 1959, the latest to be firmly dated though some of the Coast Lines posters may have been produced in the early 1960s. Rodmell had of course produced posters pre-war for various constituent companies of the latter, Burns and Laird, British and Irish, Ulster Imperial Line and the City of Cork Steam Packet Company. In the latter case an example is dated as early as 1921.

There was a long association with the General Steam Navigation Co. from c. 1924 to 1953; the last a poster advertising special cruises in the **Royal Sovereign** to view the Coronation Spithead Review in June that year. There was a long established connection with Hull where G.S.N. had an office almost from their foundation in 1824. In 1841 they bought the vessels of the bankrupt Humber Union Steam Packet Co. which they continued to run in the Hull-London coastwise service for cargo and passengers. The G.S.N. Co's office in Hull's High Street was still occupied in the 1950s when the m.v. **Auk** was working into Hull twice a week. This vessel features in a number of simple black and white adverts designed for magazines and newspapers. Similar miscellaneous graphic work was done for Bergen Line, Euxine Shipping Co., Coastlines etc but poster and shipping work effectively dries up by the 1960s.

His interest in Hull's Maritime Museum remained close and not only did he design the cover (featuring a Humber keel) for the new edition of the catalogue in 1948[42] he also helped to correct and amend the contents. There was a rich treasure trove of marine paintings by the nineteenth century Hull artists such as John Ward, Henry Redmore and many others and an outstanding collection of ship models.

Rodmell himself had made a number of models over the years to help him with the understanding of masts and rigging and to be able to appreciate a boat's form from all angles. An article from the **Boys Own** in 1919 refers to a series of models on the scale of fifty feet to one inch "with not too much detail, to help me in my work as a marine artist". The miniature fleet comprised ten items, a submarine, trawler, minesweeper, HMS **Alfridi**, (destroyer), a naval oiltanker, HMS **Legion**, (L class destroyer) SS **Defender**, HMS **Active**, (light cruiser), HMS **Tiger** (battle cruiser), HMS **King George V** (battleship) and H.M. Hospital Ship **Aquitania**. The artist goes on, "wood is the chief material used in the construction of these small ships and pins of various sizes also play a big part. The masts of the **Aquitania** are made of old knitting needles, and the big guns of the warships are bicycle spokes cut into short lengths. The tools I use are the simplest, consisting of a very sharp penknife, a one inch chisel, small plane and vice" (pl89; an illustration on the following page is dated 1919). Two other models are now in the collection of the Hull Maritime Museum, the **Ethel** a full-rigged ship of 1860, which he originally lent in 1947 and a Humber keel which he named **Dorothy Thelma** in honour of his wife.

Increasingly he occupied himself with local art groups and teaching. In addition to evening classes for the Hornsea Evening Institute he undertook day schools and weekend schools. He showed work at the local artists exhibition at the Ferens Art Gallery in 1948 and in the same year judged the ship section for the Hull Model Exhibition. Several of his watercolours were reproduced in the **Northern Review** in September that year. In 1949 he adjudicated the second Annual Exhibition of the Haltemprice Art Group, held at the Anlaby School, April 28-30. The Society had been founded by an old friend, Frank Armstrong, in 1939, had lapsed in 1941 because of the war but was reformed in 1946. Armstrong was a popular topographical artist whose work was often featured in the **Dalesman** magazine. [43]

For the fourth annual exhibition of the S.M.A. in 1949, held again at the Guildhall Gallery in London, Allanson Hick was also one of the exhibitors as was Walter Goodin (1907-1992) a Hull born artist, and protégé of Fred Elwell R.A. His subjects included portraits, landscapes, equestrian studies and still lifes. A selection from the London hanging was displayed at the Ferens Art Gallery in Hull in 1947 and 1949. 1949 also saw Rodmell submitting work to the R.A., Royal Watercolour Society and the Yorkshire Artists Exhibition at the Leeds Art Gallery. His RA contributions were two watercolours 'Marrick Priory- Swaledale' and ' Merchantmen.'

In May that year the Hull Art Club held its first post-war exhibition in the newly reopened entrance hall and mezzanine of the Ferens Art Gallery under the restored glass 'dome' which had suffered war damage. Founded in 1932 by Tom Somerscales and S H Priestman the president of the H.A.C. was Fred Elwell RA and Vincent Galloway the Director of the Ferens Art Gallery, himself a portrait

Study for Orient Line poster (30 in x 19 in).

*Study for Orient Line poster; the **Orcades** and **Orion** (30 in x 19 in).*

*Original pen drawing of the **C.A. Larsen**, whale factory ship, contrasted with the sailing whaler **Harpooner**, derived from model in the Hull Maritime Museum. Published in the **Hull Daily Mail**, 14 April 1927 and then in **Geographical Review** 1929 (12 x 19 in).*

Part of the exhibition of shipping publicity in the Hull City Hall, 1929; two large General Steam Navigation posters are prominently displayed, also many of the Humber Traders series of drawings.

painter, the vice-president. Rodmell continued his regular contributions to the Local Artists Exhibition, and in 1951 he also showed at the Victoria Park Museum, Keighley, and the Hull Art Club again as well of course at the annual exhibition of the RSMA in London.

In 1952 he designed new labels for the Sailors Orphanage collection boxes and for the pin-on flags given to street donors. 1952 also saw the production of a poster for British Railways advertising the North Sea Services of Associated Humber Lines, a poster for the General Steam Navigation Co. in 1953 and two further posters were produced in 1955 and 1959, for A.H.L. This was the last datable poster he ever produced, the first having been published thirty nine years before. Also for British Railways was a leaflet for Christmas 1952 and New Year 1953 with details of seasonal alterations in train services, illustrated with a representation of a toy-like locomotive, a parcel with a sprig of holly and a guard blowing his whistle!

Several drawings were reproduced in the **Northern Review** in 1953 and in the **Dalesman** including a pencil drawing of Keld (Swaledale) which dated from 1947 and he once again adjudicated for the Haltemprice Art Group.

Still giving his support to the Sailors Orphanage he judged a children's painting competition held in conjunction with the 1954 Whit Monday Carnival.

In November 1955 he gave a talk and demonstration for the Haltemprice Art Group at the New School, Anlaby, and in February the same year had exhibited at the Doncaster Art Club Exhibition. A commission was completed for the Association of Fish Meal Manufacturers, a series of pen drawings of trawlers of various periods employed in an advertising campaign which ran through 1955-56. His painting entitled **Windjammer** which had been displayed at the RSMA and the Ferens Art Gallery was on 28th November 1956 presented to the Lord Mayor of Hull to raise funds to help the refugees from the Hungarian uprising. It was raffled at a shilling a ticket and £84 was raised.[44] This painting can be seen in **Press On**, the journal of the Kingston Engraving Co. Ltd of Hull and appeared with a reproduction of a cargo vessel from an advertisement for Websters paint along with a brief biographical note on the artist.

As a result of an introduction by Ern Shaw he produced a number of full colour pictures for Tower Press to use as subjects for their jigsaws. A number of proofs survive and subjects include the s.s. **United States** at New York, the liner **Queen Elizabeth** as well as recreated historical scenes featuring medieval sailing craft and harbour and dock scenes both real and imaginary. [45]

His teaching activities in Hornsea had borne tremendous fruit in the decade following the war and in the local artists' exhibition held at the Ferens in 1956 no less than nineteen Hornsea artists contributed. During that year, Rodmell was Hon. Secretary of the Hull Art Club and Allanson Hick his friend and fellow marine painter was Hon. Treasurer. He adjudicated at the November exhibition of the Bridlington Art Society.

The city staged a Danish week, the Hull Anglo-Danish Festival 6-13 July, 1957, and Rodmell produced a design for the cover of the programme of events and exhibition catalogue, featuring the Hull city arms of three crowns and a Viking longship with Danish cross on the sail, the whole executed in red and white. The same design, much reduced, appeared on the adhesive advertising labels announcing the exhibition at the Hull City Hall.

Three works, "Burton Constable", "Marton" and "Wollaton Hall, Nottingham" were exhibited at the RI in Piccadilly in 1957 and he was elected a member that same year an honour which gave him a great deal of satisfaction; he submitted four subjects the following year. As the volume of commercial work decreased he found more time to paint subjects of his own choice and in a manner increasingly removed from the finely detailed studies often demanded by clients 'where every port-hole must be shown'. A favourite means of pictorial expression was line and wash, either drawing the subject first and then adding the wash, or applying the watercolour first and then drawing over it.

A combination of both techniques might be used together, along with more than one sort of line on the same sketch, perhaps drawing with a carbon pencil and adding detail in pen and ink. He gave a brief account of his approach in **The Artist**, December 1961, pp 74-6 in which he makes the following observation "Line, in one form or another, usually provides the basis of most of my work either in watercolour or oils, and although it may not appear evident at first glance, it is a fact that most of my pictures start as drawings made either with pen, pencil, chalk or brush. In the latter instance, the brush is used as a point medium in order to commence with a vigorously drawn line". (See appendix).

The arrival of acrylic paint on the artistic scene was welcomed by Rodmell and in the latter years when his hands were not as supple as they had once been the new medium was much more fluid and easier to work than oils. He used acrylic paints in a diluted form which provided an ideal medium for an artist working with Rodmell's rapidity to produce pictures resembling watercolour drawings. These are often freely executed in a loose and confident manner which is never a substitute for lack of technique but an illustration of the freedom which years of disciplined work can allow the mature artist who knows his subject matter intimately. Sixty works from members of the RSMA were shown at the Ferens in 1958, including Rodmell's "**Britannia** in the Humber" and he continued his active involvement with the Hull Art Club and Haltemprice Art Group. He gave a demonstration of watercolour painting to the latter in 1959 and the following year became Vice President. A series of one-day painting schools were sponsored by the E.R.C.C. Education Committee at Longcroft School in Beverley during 1961 and he took charge of a joint weekend painting school with the Sheffield Royalist Art Group and Chesterfield Art Club, sponsored by the Carnegie Trust, and held in the Ridgeway district. The following year he judged the art section of the Bridlington Youth Arts Festival and gave a cup bearing his name to be competed for by the Haltemprice Art Group. 1963 saw the first residential painting school at Hornsea and he gave a demonstration to the Bridlington Art Society at the public library and adjudicated for the Federation of Women's Institutes art exhibition at St. Williams College, York.

He was tutor for numerous weekend painting schools at Sheffield, Doncaster, Lincoln, Nottingham, Newark, Melton Mowbray, Shrewsbury, Ludlow, Hereford, Wolverhampton, Darlington and York, some of which he visited three times or more. The location of these courses turned his attention increasingly to landscape and architectural subjects which he more and more often exhibited though never laying aside his marine painting. Again he never failed to join in local community enterprises and regularly exhibited at the shows held by the Friends of Beverley Minster, a proportion of the proceeds from each of the pictures sold going to the restoration fund.

The Sailors Orphanage benefited in the ways we have described elsewhere and his medieval ship design for the front cover of **Magpie** the magazine of his old school at Craven Street was used by Malet Lambert school, its successor until 1969. The current guide to the parish church of St. Nicholas, Hornsea, also has a cover designed by Rodmell, the dedication to the patron saint of sailors enabling him to introduce a ship into the design.

For the 21st exhibition of the Hull Art Club he exhibited "Tiger Lane" and "Gale Force 8". The latter was exhibited at the RSMA annual exhibition the same year (1964) and was purchased for the collections of the National Maritime Museum. He also showed at the York Art Society, November 1964, and all three works submitted were accepted for the "Britain in Watercolour" exhibition held at the gallery of the Federation of British Artists in Suffolk Street.

In 1965 he judged entries for the Bridlington and District Art Society at the Town Hall, Bridlington, and participated with a watercolour entitled "Lincoln Cathedral from Brayford Wharf', in an exhibition of British work at Richmond, Virginia, organised by the Arts Exhibitions Bureau and another exhibition touring Britain under the auspices of the F.B.A.

For Brook Motors Ltd of Huddersfield he had painted a series of twelve historic ships for their 1963 Calendar which was followed in 1965 by twelve pictures of historic aircraft from biplanes to jets. Although aircraft had appeared as incidentals in some of the naval scenes produced in 1914-18 for the illustrated magazines this was the first and only time he painted them as a main subject though he had familiarised himself with their forms and silhouettes as a member of the Observer Corps in the last war. A number of full colour covers were prepared for the **Austin** magazine, 1958-1963, depicting harbour scenes and views of historic towns such as York and Lincoln.

Voyages with his wife along the coast of Norway in 1967 and 1968 filled a sketchbook which provided the basis for a number of marine studies in Rodmell's most accomplished manner; including 'North Norway' (1970) and 'Vesterälen at Brønnøysund' (ca. 1979). The latter exhibits a considerable looseness and freedom which in 'Hammerfest, northernmost town in the world', a townscape rendered in dilute acrylic, moves towards abstraction. Rodmell also enjoyed holidaying in the Yorkshire Dales with his wife, and a number of topographical paintings, again particularly watercolours, were exhibited in the 1950s and 1960s. He also provided a number of the drawings of country scenes for the **Dalesman**, to which his friend Frank Armstrong was also a regular contributor. Like Rodmell he also was captivated by ships and the sea and exhibited marine studies with the SMA and in the local artists' exhibitions in Hull and various local galleries.

Maintaining the links with the Sailors Children's Society he provided a design for their 1966 Christmas Card featuring the old floating chapel **Valiant**. He received a silver trophy for a watercolour of the oil-rig Endeavour in Bridlington Bay which he had submitted to the local artists exhibition in Bridlington. 1967 saw Rodmell on the hanging committee of the Darlington Arts Society for an exhibition at Middlesbrough Art Gallery.

Perhaps his last major commercial order was for a series of drawings with washes to illustrate a colour supplement entitled 'Britain's Third Port' which appeared in **RCH**, the house magazine of Reckitt and Colman (**RCH**, 1967, Vol. 9 No. 1, pp25-40). These were also reproduced as individual prints and sold in aid of the RNLI and the Missions to Seamen.

*Christmas Greetings originally published in the **Hull Daily Mail**, 1928 and reproduced in the brochure for the Exhibition of Ships and Humour, 1929 at the Hull City Hall (11in x 8 ¹/₂ in; page size).*

*Linocut of HMS **Nile** (1862); signed and dated 1934 (8 in x 6 in picture area).*

Greetings card for Christmas 1937; a note (below left-hand corner) indicates that the original design was displayed the same year in London at Society of Graphic Art exhibition. (10 in x 6 ½ in).

*Pen and wash drawing; drawn a number of years after the artist had made his original sketches of the **Berengaria (Imperator)** at Jarrow in 1938 (15 ¼ in x 24 ¼ in).*

In 1968 he again received a silver trophy for best exhibit at the local artists exhibition held at the Bridlington Art Gallery (Sewerby Hall) - this was a piece entitled "Beam Sea Roll". The same year he was featured in Unilever's **Port Sunlight Magazine**, a brief biographical note and an illustration of the artist at work on a canvas depicting trawlers in the Princes dock, Hull, followed by a series of pen drawings. These comprised a Palm line vessel at Bromborough Dock, Port Sunlight Wharf, The Dell, Bridge Cottage, the training centre of Unilever Merseyside Ltd., Lady Lever Art Gallery and Lever House, Ward Street.

Rodmell's 1970 contribution to the Hull Art Circle exhibition "**Britannia** and HMS **Malcolm**" was shown at the Ferens in June 1970 and then at the RSMA where it was accepted as the artists diploma piece for the society. An exhibition was held at the Vernon Gallery in 1970 to celebrate the first anniversary of the opening of the venue. Entitled "Four Yorkshire Artists " it displayed the work of Allanson Hick, Angus Rands, and the late Frank Armstrong and Harry Hudson Rodmell.

Once again in 1971 he was adjudicator for the Bridlington Art Society but advancing age was beginning to have its effect after more than fifty years of artistic endeavour and active involvement in the local community. He took the decision to hand over the accumulation of a lifetime's work as a poster designer and graphic artist to the Hull Museum, a magnificent collection comprising many hundred items.

Building on the tremendously active and enthusiastic following Rodmell had attracted through his art classes a meeting was held in October 1968, attended by some thirty people, which established the Hornsea Art Society; Harry Rodmell was duly elected president. Their first exhibition was held at the Vernon Gallery in 1971 when seventy works were hung. Some five or more of his marine and landscape subjects were hung at the Wakefield Art Gallery in an exhibition entitled "Yorkshire Scene."

The following year, 1972, he was unable to attend the second annual exhibition of the Hornsea Art Society and he also gave up his classes after some twenty-eight years as a part time teacher. In 1945 he had been invited to teach adult art classes at the East Riding Evening Institute (now the Hornsea Institute of Further Education) and continued to give three classes a week until his resignation. He did however submit work for the Hull Art Circle and the exhibition of the Friends of Beverley Minster. The third Hornsea Art Society Exhibition took place at the Vernon Gallery in 1972 and he was able to adjudicate for the Bridlington Art Society. An exhibition paying tribute to the work of his old friend Allanson Hick

was also staged in Hornsea. A biographical article published in the **Dalesman** in 1974, surprisingly, was the only account of the Rodmell's career of any substance published in his lifetime.[46]

He had been intermittently supplying both line drawings and full colour illustrations for the **Dalesman** over many years. These later included pen and wash studies of the Hull docks, Scarborough harbour, Flamborough village, Stone Creek (Patrington), some as cover designs, others internally, the larger scenes as a double spread. The cover design for May 1975 was the Saturday Market, Beverley, for August 1975, Paull Lighthouse and in July 1977 one of the Hull - New Holland steam paddle ferries. Pen drawings included Bridlington harbour, Blacktoft, Whitby, the Whitby Pickering railway, Staithes and Wansford near Driffield. In 1965 his drawing of the **S.S. Duke of Clarence** originally published in the **Hull Daily Mail**, 1925, was also reproduced in the **Dalesman** following a reader's query. A book entitled **Yorkshire Ports and Harbours** issued by Dalesman publications in 1967 includes a colour illustration entitled "Timber Dock at Hull".

Rodmell's dear old friend, Allanson Hick died in 1975 and he was already ailing. His two pieces 'Dockland' and 'Lighthouse Pier' in 1974 were the last to be shown at the R.S.M.A's annual exhibition. He was of course a founder member and had been active on the committee for fifteen years as well as designing the society's insignia in 1949. This is in the form of a medieval ship with an artist's palette and brush representing the sail and mast.

Though his reputation amongst fellow artists was high and his work was eagerly sought by collectors the public at large were little aware of his contribution to the art of the poster and to the great British tradition of marine painting. In 1979 the Royal Society of Marine Artists acknowledged his long service to the society and his stature as a marine artist by making Rodmell an Honorary member.

Sadly he was unable to complete his canvas entitled "Storm Force 10", depicting a trawler battling through fiercely raging seas, which he had intended to show at the 10th Hornsea Art Society exhibition in 1980. By this time the society which he had founded was a thriving organisation with some eighty to ninety practising artists. One of his last canvases was a scene of trawlers fitting out in Hull's Princes Dock, entitled "Domes, Masts and Funnels" which he painted for the new fishing gallery of the Town Docks Museum, opened in 1976. This was the second phase of a complete redisplay of the city's maritime collection in the magnificent Dock Offices of 1871. Unfortunately he was unable to attend the official opening and he never was able to visit the new establishment which would have been a surprising contrast to the Aladdin's cave jumble of the old fisheries museum he had known so well.

In 1981 he contributed to the wedding album presented by the RI to Prince Charles and Lady Diana Spencer for their wedding, the artist's last public contribution.

Plans were well under way for a retrospective exhibition to be held at the Town Docks Museum utilising both the marvellous graphic works he had presented and a cross section of watercolours and oils lent by local collectors.[47] Sadly, Harry Rodmell died 3 March 1984 but the exhibition went ahead as a memorial to one of Britain's finest marine artists, and was officially opened by Terence Storey, the then Vice-President of the R.S.M.A.

Harry Rodmell was a commercial artist of great professional skill and one of the outstanding poster makers of his generation. He was also a first class watercolourist, and artist in the full sense of that word. He was constantly developing and eagerly embraced new materials, finding acrylic a medium which suited the looser style of his mature years. The more detailed ship portraits were abandoned in favour of imaginative studies created from memory and his sketch book jottings. At the very end of his career he produced a number of abstracts which are the logical conclusion of his increasingly free approach to painting but for a man in his late seventies are remarkable for their vivid colour and sheer verve.

Throughout his entire career as a professional artist he worked from a studio in his native Yorkshire, near the coast at Hornsea. He visited London for RSMA shows and the like but never spent any great length of time there.

His knowledge of ships came from close observation of the huge variety of vessels which visited the Hull docks or were seen in the Humber and along the East Coast. Sketches and notes were supplemented by a mass of cuttings and extracts from magazines which he collected all his life and if necessary by photographs from the commissioning company to provide information not otherwise available. His own voyages were few and, despite having produced such a marvellous array of posters advertising liner services and cruises around the world, were restricted to the North Sea.

The great tradition of marine art in Hull and East Yorkshire continues with a number of artists whose work has achieved international renown. Colin Verity, who wrote an obituary of Harry Rodmell which appeared in the **Times**[48] continues

Rodmell's work with the Hornsea Art Society and is their president. Steven Dews though now living in the South of England has produced some outstanding work especially attractive being those of the great J and K class yachts. D.C. Bell working in rural Lincolnshire, though primarily a marine artist, has also produced fine studies of aircraft and locomotives too and published (in 1982) a collection of drawings and watercolours with the title **Britain's Maritime History - an illustrated chronical**.

The Rodmell archive held in the Hull Maritime Museum contains an example of practically every major and minor piece of graphic art produced by the artist. This comprises printed posters, studies for posters, pen drawings and hundreds of proofs of miscellaneous illustrations and advertisements. Over the last decade a trickle of posters have appeared in the sale rooms, both in the north and in London and examples of his work have been lent from the museum for major exhibitions including "Art on the Liners - a Celebration of Elegance at Sea", Southampton City Art Gallery, in 1986[49] and "Schip & Affiche" at the Prins Hendrik Maritime Museum, Rotterdam, in 1987.[50] Examples of his posters are in the Robert Opie collection,[51] and posthumously in 1990 Suntory of Japan used Rodmell's image of the **Normandie** on a poster advertising their "Crest" and "Royal" brands of whisky. [52]

Christmas card designed for the Royal Observer Corp. 1941 (6 1/4 in x 4 3/4 in).

Associated Humber Line; the M.V. **Fountains Abbey,** *launched 1954; 1955 (Published by British Railways N.E. Regions 55. Printed in Great Britain, Nathaniel Lloyd and Co. Ltd, London SE1).*

Pen and wash drawing of the four-masted bark **Olivebank***; signed. Reproduction from the RCH magazine 1967.*

CHRONOLOGY

1896 — Born 28th May and christened Harry Hudson Rodmell; his father averring that if he was christened Henry he would be called Harry anyway!

1912 — Entered Hull School of Art.

1919 — Demobilised from the Royal Engineers after war service. Engaged by Ronald Massey, artists' agent.

1923 — Illustrations for D.W. Bone, **The Lookoutman**.

1925-1929 — Drawings of 'Humber Traders' in the **Hull Daily Mail**

1926 — Brochure entitled "This Year Belgium via Hull-Zeebrugge" illustrated in collaboration with Ern Shaw.

1927-30 — Drawing of 'Guardships of the Humber' in the **Hull Daily Mail**. The 'Menin Gate', 25 July 1927 ditto.

1929 — January-February; Victoria Galleries, Carr Lane, Shipping Publicity material; exhibited with Ern Shaw's pieces in 'Foilacq', a technique involving the use of aluminium foil, lacquer and oils.

1935 — Hull Art Circle, Ferens Art Gallery; the **Mauretania**.

1936 — Elected to the Society of Graphic Art.

1937 — Elected Fellow of the Royal Society of Arts.

Painting of **s.s. Mauretania** shown in the Sea Power Exhibition

1939 — Invited by Charles Pears to join a group of marine artists, later known as the Society of Maritime Artists.

1940 — United Artists Exhibition, Burleigh House, London.

1943 — Marries Dorothy Thelma Fisher.

1946 — November-December; inaugural exhibition of the Society of Marine Artists.

1949 — Summer Exhibition of the Royal Academy, watercolours entitled 'Merchantman' and 'Marrick Priory, Swaledale'. SMA touring exhibition at the Ferens Art Gallery.

Yorkshire Artists Exhibition; Leeds Art Gallery. Hull Art Circle; first post-war exhibition. Royal Institute of Painters in Watercolours; annual exhibition in London.

1955 — 'Evolution of British Deep Sea Trawlers, 1853-1955', advertising campaign for Association of Fish Meal Manufacturers.

1957 — Elected member of the Royal Institute of Painters in Watercolour.

1967 — Illustrations for 'The Third Port', supplement to RCH, Reckitt and Colman's house magazine.

1970 — Hull Art Circle, Ferens Art Gallery; oil entitled 'Royal Occasion', later selected as diploma piece for RSMA. RSMA touring exhibition, Rotherham; 'Royal Occasion'. Four Yorkshire Artists': Allanson Hick; Angus Rands; H. Hudson Rodmell; Frank Armstrong; at the Vernon Gallery, Hornsea, April-May.

1971 — First exhibition of the Hornsea Art Society at the Vernon Gallery, Hornsea. Gift of shipping publicity material to the Hull Museum.

1973 — Gift of shipping photographs and cuttings to the National Maritime Museum, Greenwich.

1976 — Acrylic painting 'Domes, Masts and Funnels', for the Town Docks Museum.

1977 — Watercolour entitled '**Berengaria's** last berth' given to the Ferens Art Gallery.

1981 — Contributes to album of watercolours assembled by the Royal Institute of Painters in Watercolour for a wedding gift to Prince Charles and Lady Diana Spencer.

1984 — Died on the 3rd March, aged 87.

NOTES

1. Henry Rodmell died aged 60, 11 May, 1923, at 3 Melrose Villa, Wilton Road, Hornsea.

2. A school of art was founded in 1861 to teach applied art and industrial design. Originally situated in the Public Rooms (Kingston Square) it transferred in 1878 to 2 Albion Street when it became affiliated to the Hull Literary and Philosophical Society, and then in 1895 became part of the Municipal Technical School. New premises were built in 1905 to the design of Lanchester, Stewart and Rickards, situated on the Anlaby road backing onto the railway station and Station Hotel. See A.G. Credland **Marine Painting in Hull Through Three Centuries**, Hull 1993, p 8 and R. Barnard **A History of Further Education in Hull**, Hull 1996, pp 124-130; and **Eastern Morning News**, 7 and 12 October 1878.

3. James Robert Granville Exley (1878-1967). Born at Great Horton, Bradford, attended Bradford Grammar School and studied at Skipton Science and Art Schools and the Royal College of Art where he received his diploma in 1907. Elected ARE in 1905, RE in 1923. Deputy Head Master of Ryland Memorial Municipal School of Art in 1909, Principal of the Cambridge and County Schools of Arts and Crafts (1909-1912), and Head Master of the City of Hull Municipal School of Art (1912-1919). Lived latterly at Grassington, Yorks.

4. No. 1 issued 1914, no. 2 in 1916 and no. 3 after the end of the war in 1919. One of his fellow students was George F. Holmes a founder member of the Humber Yawl Club in 1883 who provided an etching entitled Winteringham Haven for the 1919 folio; Rodmell's etching was titled 'Ready Aye Ready'. Loosely inserted in the folio is a small etching of warships inscribed to H. Rodmell Esq. From George F. Holmes.

It is interesting to note that the cover of folio 1 was a design of a medieval vessel with the sail represented by an artist's palette which is clearly an early prototype for the insignia of the Royal Society of Marine Artists.

5. A summary account of his education in the City of Hull Municipal School of Art, Anlaby road, appears in a report, written by J.R.G. Exley, the principal. This was appended to the minutes of the Higher Education Sub-Committee, 14 January 1919. In conclusion, Exley draws the committee's attention to the value of the 'art scholarship' which proved so fruitful in this case, and also the problem which arose with individuals who continued their education after 14 years of age thus de-barring many from taking up an apprenticeship in an appropriate trade.

6. **ibid**.

7. **ibid**.

8. Of 23 Knightrider Street, EC4 and later 106 and 108 Victoria Street. SW1; 1946 Carew, Wilson, Massey Ltd. WC2.

9. Sir David Bone (1884-1959) served in the Anchor Line of which he became Commodore. His exciting career is related in his own publications, **The Brassbounder** (1910), **Merchantman-at'Arms** (1919) and **Merchantman Re-armed**, (1949). The last two were illustrated by his brother Muirhead Bone. Rodmell gave to the museum a second impression, 1924, signed on the flyleaf 'presented by Mr. H. Hudson Rodmell to the Museum of Fisheries and Shipping'. His personal book label is pasted on the following page.

10. Probably George F. Holmes.

11. Miss Jacobs; Louise Rice Jacobs ARCA (1890-1946). Cartoonist, portrait and landscape artist. One woman show in 1925 at the Hull Municipal Gallery, sometime secretary of Hull Arts and Crafts Society. Latterly lived at New Malden, Surrey. Exhibited widely, including R.A. A portrait of Benno Pearlman when Lord Mayor, hangs in the Hull Guildhall.

12. A cartoon illustration entitled 'Modern Hull dresses her window at Wembley' appeared in the **Hull Daily Mail** 2 June 1925 p6. Depicted among the various items characterising the city's trade and commerce is a sketch of the brochure cover.

13. A description of the frieze, fifty yards long, eight feet deep, appears in the **Hull Daily Mail** 22 June, 1925, p3. The photograph of a thirty-foot section shows the Hull docks, vessels at their berths with cranes alongside, all within an architectural frame. The frame included images of seed-crushing, shipbuilding, fishing, timber, milling, cement manufacture, fruit imports, engineering, colours and paint-making etc. The colours for the painting were supplied by the local paint manufacturers Blundell and Spence. A note in the **Museums Journal**, Wed. 26 January, 1927, tells us that the panels illustrate the following commodities and the Hull industries beneath them; oils, paints and varnishes, fishing, grain, milling, shipping, fruit and vegetables, cement, seed-crushing, timber, warehousing etc.

14. See 'Guide to the Museum of Commerce and Transport' **Hull Museum Publication** no. 180, Hull, 1935, (edited by Thomas Sheppard); Thomas Sheppard **Hull's Shop Window**, Hull, n.d.; and **The City and Port of Hull**, 1932 esp. p.47.

15. See **Hull Daily Mail**, 11 January 1927, p3.

16. See **Hull Daily Mail**, 20 June, 1926 p3; and **Hull Daily Mail** 28 September, 1926, p3. A beneficiary of this tradition was Molly Moss; born in Hull, she attended the Hull Art School in 1931 and later exhibited in London. She was a member of the Hampstead Artists Council and certainly produced at least one poster design for the London Underground, in 1950.
A contemporary of Rodmell's was Kathleen Tyson (Mrs. Mawer 1898-1983) who studied at Grimsby and Hull School of Art then at Westminster School of Art. A landscape and miniature painter she was elected S.W.A. 1939; was a member of the Society of Marine Artists from 1940. Exhibited ROI, RBA, RA, NEAC etc.

17. See appendix (1).

18. See appendix (2).

19. Rodmell gave to the Museum of Fisheries and Shipping one of six albums containing prints pulled from the blocks of this series, a total of fifty images.

20. 4 January, p6; 8 January, p9 and 14 January, p8. (**Hull Daily Mail**, 1926).

21. The originals were donated to Hull Museums and in 1940-1942 were reproduced in the **Seafarer** magazine, courtesy of Thomas Sheppard, the curator.

22. During the war years he lived at 6 St. Nicholas Mount, Newbegin, Hornsea.

23. See **Commercial Art** 1929, pp. 233-240; the Rodmell poster is reproduced in vol. 8, 1939, p.82.

24. Died aged 95 in the Hull Royal Infirmary, 22 February 1986. Born in Bean Street, Hull, the youngest of twelve children he attended the Day Street school and after several temporary jobs became a travelling salesman for a drapers. Encouraged initially by his teachers he eventually decided to take a correspondence course in drawing run by Percy V. Bradshaw of the Press Art School. He gained a position in the **Hull Evening News** and for the next twenty years produced a stream of cartoons and illustrations for that newspaper and the **Sports Express** and also began to send material to several national publications. During the first war he was a member of the Royal Army Medical Corps based at Reading where he was staff artist for the hospital magazine. Before the last war Ern Shaw broadcast a weekly comic feature on the north regional radio called 'Radiosities'. Author of several comic annuals he also published **How to become a sucessful cartoonist** (London, 1946). His last publication was **Pocket Puzzle Pie** issued in 1977 when he was 86 and he was also in these later years providing puzzles for TV programmes such as 'Ask the Family'. He was an honorary life member of the Cartoonists Club of Great Britain. See the **Cottingham Review**, 2 May 1953, p3 and **Hull Daily Mail** 24 February, 1986, p3.

25. None of these venues has been confirmed; no record has been discovered in the archives of the various provincial galleries. However there was an 'Exhibition of advertising art' by the British Society of Poster Designers which was staged at Derby 5 August - 7 September 1927. The catalogue (not illustrated) has an introduction by Percy V. Bradshaw, author of **Art in Advertising** etc. The exhibits were predominantly posters for the various railway companies (mainly the LNER); twenty-three artists were represented **not** including Rodmell whose name is also absent from the list of members of the society, whose president was Frank Brangwyn (later to be Hon. V.P. of the R.S.M.A.). H.G. Gawthorne, Frank Newbould, Charles Pears (founder of the R.S.M.A.), Norman Wilkinson, K.D. Shoesmith, Odin Rosenvinge, Tom Purvis were all members whose work was included in the display. I am indebted to Maggie Cullen, Keeper of Fine Arts, Derby Art Gallery, for bringing this to my attention.

26. **Commercial Art**, vol. XII, 1932, pl. 91.

27. **Commercial Art and Industry**, 1933, p.204.

28. Opened July 1937 by the Rt. Hon. Winston Churchill at the New Burlington Galleries. See A.G. Credland 'The Royal Society of Marine Artists, 1939-1995', an essay in **A Celebration of Marine Art-Fifty Years of the Royal Society of Marine Artists**, London, 1996, pp. 147-153.

29. See **Daily Express** June, 1934.

30. **Smedwick Telephone**, 27 October, 1934.

31. **Hull Daily Mail** 24 November 1978.

32. **Hull Daily Mail** 28 January 1939.

33. **Hull Daily Mail** 28 December 1939.

34. Arthur G. Credland **Allanson Hick, Architect and Artist, 1898-1975**, Hull, 1991, 60pp.

35. Archives of the Royal Society of Marine Artists.

36. Catalogue of the **United Artists Exhibition**, Royal Academy of Arts, London, 1940.

37. At 6 Melrose Villas, Wilton Road, Hornsea in the 1920s. See note 22.

38. **The Second United Artists Exhibition**, Royal Academy, 1942 and The **Third United Artists Exhibition, R.A.**, 1943.

39. No catalogue of the inaugural exhibition has been located by the present author but **Sea Breezes**, vol. 3, 1947 pp. 56-7 lists the artists who contributed.

40. Catalogues of the annual exhibition **passim** and R.S.M.A. archives.

41. In 1949 he was living at 68 Cliff Road, Hornsea. Latterly he and his wife occupied 'Arncliffe' a house at Atwick on the outskirts of Hornsea. See notes 22 and 37.

42. Amongst the material in the Rodmell archive there are several alternative studies, one showing a full-rigged ship in profile, another a whaleship in the ice, the third the P.S. **Wilberforce** with the three crowns of the Hull coat of arms overlaid. The chosen cover was used for all subsequent editions of the catalogue-cum-guide until the closure of the Fisheries and Shipping Museum in 1974.

43. Frank Armstrong F.R.S.A. published a number of volumes reproducing his sketches: **Hull and District SketchBook**, 1953; **Yorkshire Sketchbook**, 1963 and Sketches of **Yorkshire Landmarks**, Clapham via Lancaster, 1967. The latter was published shortly after his death with a text by H.J. Scott editor of the **Dalesman** and reproduced a selection of his topographical pieces from that periodical. He collapsed whilst giving one of his illustrated talks and died, aged 66, the next morning at his home (24 Lowfield Road, Anlaby).

44. In 1966 it went to a local auction house and was purchased by G.K. Beaulah, a Hull collector. He also had a scraperboard of Rodmell's depicting cobles at South Landing, Flamborough, and a lino-cut of HMS **Nile** (1862), executed in 1934.

45. These included a boatyard scene, catamaran, yachts in full sail, cargo ship berthing, the **Queen Elizabeth** in New York harbour, **Queen Elizabeth** berthing, tugs and ferries in New York harbour, the m.v. **United States** accompanied by tugs, a Hull trawler bringing in its net, Cornish harbour scene, a cruise liner in the tropics, fishing boats and pleasure steamer in harbour, aerial view of cargo vessel; also Tudor ships (a castle in the background), a river scene with stone bridge and pleasure boats, and sheep crossing a stone bridge.

46. Jack Whitfield, ' Harry Hudson Rodmell: an outstanding marine artist', **Dalesman**, August 1982, pp. 379-381.

47. A.G. Credland **Harry Hudson Rodmell, RI R.S.M.A., Marine Artist, 1896-1984,** Hull, 1984. Publication to accompany exhibition; bulletin No. 16, Hull Museums and Art Galleries.

48. **The Times**, 13 March, 1984; see also **Hull Daily Mail**, 6 March, 1984 and (Holderness) **Gazette**, 9 March, 1984.

49. 17 May - 29 June.

50. See the accompanying publication **Schip en Affiche** with contributions by Tanjer de Boer; Cassandra Bosters, Ed. De Heer, Rudy Konsbroek, Wilma Oosterwijk and Pim Reinders, Maritiem Museum Prins Hendrik, Rotterdam 1987, 183pp. (ISBN 90 6322 1290). Two of Rodmell's Nederland Royal Mail posters are reproduced p. 146, cat. Nos. 56 and 58.

51. 'Hamburg-America Linie (HAPAG) West Indies' and 'Central America-Oceanic Steamship Company, Europe-Sydney', Robert Opie Collection, Museum of Advertising and Packaging, Gloucester.

52. This was a two-week campaign within Japan itself. The particular subject was apparently chosen because the advertising manager had happened across Rodmell's illustration of the **Normandie** in the 1935 **Shipbuilder** journal. She had a futuristic design which even now looks quite 'modern'.

A SUMMARY LIST OF COMPANIES RODMELL ACCEPTED COMMISSIONS FROM

The typical poster is **double royal** size 40in x 25in (102cm x 64cm), some are **double crown**, 30in x 20in (76cm x 51cm). Some landscape format posters are **quad royal**, 40in x 50in (102cm x 127cm). A few multi-sheet posters were produced for the General Steam Navigation Co.; one featuring the **Golden Eagle** (1920s) and another the **Crested Eagle** (1930s) each made up of two 60in x 40in sheets and a twelve sheet production advertising the **Royal Eagle** (1930s) comprising four 60in x 40in, four 40in x 40in and four sheets with lettering, 17in x 38in. Also for the G.S.N.C. is a **quad crown**, 30in x 40in (176cm x 102cm) of the **Royal Sovereign** (1950s) and another of the P.S. **Trident** and m.v. **Auk** (c. 1948). For the Ulster Imperial Line a poster of two sheets, each 60in x 40in, featuring the m.v. **Ulster Monarch**, **Ulster Queen** and **Ulster Prince** (1930s).

An asterisk indicates one or more printed posters are extant.

Shipping Companies - Britain and Ireland

Aberdeen Steam Navigation Co. Ltd c.1948.

* Associated Humber Lines 1952 - 1959.

Belfast Steamship Co 1924 and 1950s.

* British and Irish Steam Packet Co 1924 to 1950s.

B and I, Free State Lines.

British Channel Islands Shipping Co.

* B.T.D.B. (formerly B.T.C. British Transport Commission) 1950s - 1960s.

* Burns and Laird Line 1920s -1950s.

* City of Cork Steam Packet Co. Ltd 1922 - 1950s.

Coastlines Ltd 1935 - 1952.

Curry Ltd (Edinburgh).

* Eagle Steamers (see G.S.N. Co. Ltd) 1930s.

Elliot Steam Tug Co. Ltd. (Ship Towage).

Gamecock Tugs (Ship Towage).

* General Steam Navigation Co. Ltd 1920s - 1950s.

Goole Steam Shipping Co. Ltd.

Irish Free State Lines (B and I).

* David McBrayne (Glasgow) c.1938 - 1953.

* North of Scotland, Orkney and Shetland Shipping Co. Ltd. Aberdeen.

* Queen Line (New Medway Steam Packet Co.).

Ship Towage 1951 - 1968.

Tyne Tees Steam Shipping Co. Ltd 1945 etc.

* Ulster Imperial Lines (Belfast Steamship Co.) 1929 - 1950s.

William Watkins Ltd 1926 - 1950.

Miscellaneous

* Shipbuilding Conference (c.1960).

Shipping Companies - Overseas.

Aberdeen and Commonwealth Line 1929.

American Export Line.

* Atlantic Transport Line 1920 - 1930s.

Asiatic Petroleum Co. Ltd. (Shell) 1930s.

* Australian Commonwealth Line 1930s.

Batavier Line 1923 - 1930s.

* Bergen Line 1920 - 1954.

Blue Star Line 1930s.

Booth Line.

British India Line 1937 etc.

* Canadian Pacific 1921.

* Canadian Pacific Overseas Service (C.P.O.S.) 1920.

Clipper Line 1951.

Consulmar (Spain).

Cosulich Line (Trieste) 1930s.

Cunard 1950s.

Deutsche Afrika Dienst 1923.

Deutsche Ost-Afrika Linie.

D.F.D.S. (Det Forenede Dampschiffahrts Selskab) 1938-39.

* Ellerman's Wilson Line 1921 - 1930s.

Euxine Shipping Co 1953 - 1957.

* Finland Line c.1925 - 1930s.

* French Line 1920s - 1930s.

Furness Line.

Furness Philadelphia Transatlantic Lines   (Furness Withy).

Fyffes Lines.

German Africa Line c.1936.

German East Africa Lines (Deutsches Ost-Afrika/D.O.A.L.).

Greek Line 1950s - 1960s.

* Hamburg - Amerika Line (HAPAG) 1923 - 1930s.

Holland America Line 1930s.

Italia Line.

J.C.J.L.

KLM (airline) 1923.

Lamport and Holt Line 1919.

Michael Murphy Ltd. (Dublin) 1931.

* Nederland Royal Mail Co. (Royal Dutch Mail) 1930s - 1949.

* Norddeutscher Lloyd c.1923 - c.1935.

Nordenfjeldske 1930s.

* Oceanic Steamship Co. (San Francisco) 1930s.

Oranje Line.

P and O / Orient Line 1930s.

Port Line c.1923 etc.

Queen Line 1930s - 1940s.

* Royal Holland Lloyd 1921 - 1930s.

Royal Mail Line (Royal Mail Steam Packet Co.) c.1920.

* Shaw Saville Albion Line c.1925 - 1930.

SITMAR (Society Italia Trasporti Maritimi).

* Swedish American Line (Svenska Amerika Linien) 1930s.

Swedish East Asiatic Co. (Svenska - Ostasiatiska Kompaniet) Gothenburg 1929 - 1939.

* Swedish Lloyd 1930s.

Union Castle Line.

* United American Lines 1923 - 1932.

Westcott and Laurance Lines Ltd. (Ellerman Lines) 1928.

White Star Line 1921.

Wilson Line (See Ellermans).

Zeeland Steamship Co 1923.

Shipping Agents

British and Northern Shipping Agency (London) 1938.

Thomas Cook and Son Ltd (London).

Dean and Dawson c.1933.

D.H. Drakeford.

Gellatly Hankey (London).

John Good and Son Ltd. (Hull) 1920s-1930s.

P.H. Matthiessen (Newcastle) 1953.

Gustav Metzler (Stettin).

Moxon, Salt and Co. (London) 1920s.

W. H. Müller (London) c.1922 - 1923.

Wainwright Bros. and Co. (London) 1925.

Wakefield Bros. and Co. (London

West End Passenger Agents (London) 1927.

Industrial and Commercial.

Algerian Wine.
Anglo-Innes Transport Ltd.
A.S.C.M.
Asiatic Petroleum (Shell Oil)   1928.
Association of Fish Meal Manufacturers (Teddington, Beds.) 1955 - 56.
Austin Magazine 1958 - 1963.
Beechams Pills c.1920.
B.O.C. (British Oxygen Co.) 1930s.
Brook Motors Ltd. (Huddersfield) 1963 and 1965.
Cochranes Ltd. Ship Builders (Selby).
Cook, Welton and Gemmell, Shipbuilders (Beverley) 1948 etc.
Elswick and Hopper Cycles (Barton upon Humber).
Gauntlet Weather Tested Paints (Archibald Hamilton and Co. Ltd. Glasgow).
German Federal Railways.
Hall's Barton Ropery (Barton upon Humber) Lincs.
Harland and Wolff (Belfast) c.1936.
Kingston Engraving Co. Ltd. (Hull).
K.L.M. (Royal Dutch Airlines) 1950s.
Link Line Ltd.
D.W. Massey and Co. Ltd. (Hull).
Newsums of Lincoln (Manufactured Woodwork).
Northern Ireland Traders Ltd.
R. and W. Paul 1950.
Priestman Bros. (Hull).
R.A.C. 1962.
R.C.H. (Reckitt and Colman Holdings) 1967.
Shell Oil (see Asiatic Petroleum).

Shipbuilding Conference (London) c. 1960.
William Sloan and Co. Ltd.
Stather Washable Wallpapers.
John G. Stuart Ltd. Rum Importers (Edinburgh).
Websters Ltd. (Marine paints) (Hull).
W.D. and H.O. Wills (Cigarette Cards).

Railway Companies

British Railways 1952 - 1953.
German Federal Railways 1950s.
L.M.S and L.N.E.R. 1926.
* L.N.E.R poster, 'Lakeland by the Sea' c. 1930.
* Railway Executive North Eastern Railways, Associated Humber Lines.

Periodicals, Magazines and Newspapers

Argosy
Ashore and Afloat 1931 - 1952
Bystander 1917
Dalesman 1965 - 1977
Geographical Review   1929
Graphic 1920
Helmsman 1932 etc
Help Yourself Annual 1934
Hull Daily Mail 1920 - 1930 etc.
Hull Daily News 1919
Illustrated London News 1920
Joy Rays 1929
Leeds Mercury 1920s and 1930s
Magpie (school magazine) 1912 and 1932
The Motorship   1925
The New Illustrated 1919
Northern Review 1948
Pearsons
Penny Pictorial 1917
Port of Hull
Sea Breezes
Sea Breezes (magazine of Hornsea County Primary School 1952)

Seafarer 1940 -1942
Port Sunlight Magazine (Unilever) 1968
The Shipbuilder and Marine Engine Builder 1935
Shipping Wonders of the World 1936 - 1937
Sphere 1918 - 1920
Sunday Pictorial
Trade of Hull and the Humber Ports 1938 - 1943; 1946, 1947
Tyneside Industrial Review 1939
War Illustrated 1918
Wilberforce (Masonic) Lodge No 2134, Hull
Young Hull; A pictorial record of junior welfare work in Hull and district during 1924 (Souvenir of Hull Cenotaph unveiling) Sept 20, 1924

Book Plates

Armorial bookplate of John Divine M.D., A.S.F. Oliver and one designed for the author's wife. Also small decorative heraldic labels, monochrome, with artist's initials.

Books

David W Bone **The Lookoutman**, London 1923 illustrated in colour and black and white.
Proof copy of dustjacket of Jack Henry **Beyond The Rivers Mouth** c.1930.
Proof copy of dustjacket for **While The Sea Remaineth**.
Colour illustration of Timer Dock at Hull used on cover of Baron F Duckham. **Yorkshire Ports and Harbours**, Dalesman, 1967.

APPENDICES

1) Getting There as Part of the Holiday. (Hull Daily Mail 4 August 1925)

Although we are proud of calling ourselves a seafaring nation, the majority of us are not quite so sure of appearing as dignified representatives of Father Neptune when it comes to trusting ourselves to his tender care on board ship. The sea is all very well, we say, to bathe in or view from the promenade of a favourite seaside resort, but when it comes to making it a home from home it is a very different matter.

There is some truth, however, in the saying that one cannot properly appreciate the merits of one's own country until one has visited others, and apart from this no slight is cast upon the unchallenged charm and beauty of this great little island of ours in any desire to travel further afield. Yet - due no doubt to our island situation - we are apt to forget that only a few hours travel will take us to lands of complete contrast in scenery, customs, people, buildings; in fact, we find ourselves, once we have arrived, wondering why we have never plucked up the courage to visit them long ago. That is just the point. It would, perhaps, not be far wrong to say that in a great number of cases it is only the thought of that short sea crossing which has always been the obstacle, and the enthusiasm of our friends who have been over has never been quite sufficient to dispel the feelings so frequently expressed by that familiar phrase, 'I would like to go if it wasn't for the sea'.

Now even when the decision to go abroad has definitely been made, the passage across - and especially if it be a short one - is looked upon as a sort of necessary evil, merely a means of transit to be tolerated as best one can, but most certainly not part of the holiday in its true sense. This is surely a mistake, for given reasonably good conditions - and during the summer months good crossings are fairly general - a short sea voyage like one from Hull to Zeebrugge can be counted as part and parcel of the holiday, and enjoyed as such.

Anyhow, others have survived the ordeal and so we have at last booked our passage, and the time has arrived when we shall soon be able to judge for ourselves.

Good fortune seems to smile upon us at the very beginning for it is one of those serene and beautiful evenings which we do get in England in spite of the pessimists' attempts to prove otherwise, and we go along to the Riverside Quay all excitement, and proceed to make our first acquaintance with the ship - our ship, as we soon find ourselves calling her, - which is to take us over. Most people living at a seaport are on kind of nodding terms with ships from a land viewpoint, but in many cases this is their first intimate connection with anything more closely associated with 'life on the ocean waves' than the Humber Ferry or an hour on the Boating Lake, so the remarks one overhears are vastly amusing, and constitute an entertainment in themselves. However, there will be ample time to indulge and improve one's knowledge of nautical terms later, and in the meantime a courteous and smiling steward is waiting to show us our berth. This preliminary but important detail over, and we are free to take stock of our surroundings and the ship, which, as heralded by a sharp blast from the siren is on the point of departure.

Down comes the 'Blue Peter' (the flag flown by vessels in port which indicates that they are about to sail) as we glide away from the Quay side and we find ourselves really and truly commencing the first stage of our holiday.

The loud clanging of a gong announces that dinner is ready but many of our passengers, to whom the trip is an absolute novelty, prefer to stay on deck awhile in order to see all there is to see, as they say of our passage down the river. It is certainly interesting to view Britain's Third Port from the approach of her most important heritage; we are so used to entering or leaving by way of roads or station that we seldom think of what Hull looks like to those who go down to the sea in ships, and upon whose business the success of our city depends.

We have now passed the Pier and Alexandra Dock entrance with the huge structure of Earle's crane, that familiar landmark, looming up against the evening sky, just astern. The King George Dock and Salt End are passed in quick succession, and our attention is now turned towards the Lincolnshire side as we approach Immingham. Drawing nearer, a very fine vessel, with a cream funnel and rows of white promenade decks, calls for admiration and comment and much guessing goes on before we learn that she is the **Arcadian**, of the Royal Mail Line, one of the largest steamers in the world devoted exclusively to pleasure cruising. 'She doesn't look very big' someone remarks, but a large tramp steamer is just passing between us and the liner, and the latter's great bulk of 12,000 odd tons at once becomes apparent by the contrast.

The next thing to catch our eye is a huge unwieldy, irregular mass rising from the water just ahead of us and somewhat suggestive, from a distance, of one of the early, top-heavy ironclads. Conjecture to the identity of this ugly monster is wild in the extreme, and quite justifiable for the object is no ship at all but a kind of fort erected during the war in connection with the Humber defences and the boom used for the prevention of the entry of enemy shipping.

Ever and anon, as we continue our journey seaward, we pass the buoys which mark the navigable channel of the river, and as they roll about like drunken men in our wash, they emit that flat, doleful note by the clang of their bells. There seems to be no other sound quite the same.

As the river broadens out to meet the sea the transition is almost imperceptible, except for a slight feeling that our ship is making a more determined thrust against the extra weight of the long rollers of the open water.

Spurn is fast disappearing on our port quarter, and the pilot cutter of the Humber Conservancy Board can just be made out keeping her station off the Head. The **Duke of Clarence** is now well settled down to her work, and it is only as we rapidly overhaul a big tramp thrashing her way out at a steady nine knots that we realise that it is not for nothing that our little liner has earned for herself the title of 'The Flying Duke'.

Passing vessels of all kinds keep up a continual interest. Here is a trawler; she looks as though she had been away for a considerable time, so weather-beaten and covered with rust is she, and plunging along as if anxious to get home again for a brief and well-earned rest. A little later we meet another tramp, this time homeward bound in ballast, churning up the water in fine style with her propeller half showing, and sending a solid fountain of white foam nearly as high as her deck.

But it is getting dark. The twinkling lights, red, green and white, of passing traffic, and the bright white eye of a distant lightship away on our starboard bow tell of approaching night on the sea, and someone makes the pleasant suggestion that some supper in the comfortable and cheerful saloon where many of our fellow travellers are already gathered, would not be amiss.

When at last we go below to our cosy little bunk, we almost feel sorry that we are to have only one night of this new mode of living, and when we awake in the morning to find the sun turning the crests of the short jumpy waves into points of silver we are even more enthusiastic. It is still two full hours earlier than our accustomed time for rising at home, but we feel that we are missing a treat in not getting up at once.

A turn or two on the deck puts us in good humour with the whole world, and it is just this particular time at sea - the first few hours following the dawn - which makes us think of those lines of Kipling in which he so graphically expresses that ' The East wind is brewed fresh and fresh every morning.'

By now we are joined by many more of our friends of overnight, who are also bent on taking a constitutional - what a contrast to the daily dash for the office! - and we need no urging when the breakfast gong summons us to the saloon.

Returning on deck, we find all eyes and attention fixed on the distant horizon right ahead for land has been sighted and what appeared originally as a long grey indistinct smudge is rapidly assuming definite shapes, and soon we can pick out buildings and other objects, and of course everyone is trying to be the first to spot the now famous Mole.

A fleet of fishing boats is putting out to sea - a very picturesque type of craft they are, with their brown sails, and mast heads and blocks painted in a variety of different colours - and two or three big liners, amongst them a big Red Star boat from Antwerp and a Holland-Amerika Liner from Rotterdam, are passing at no great distance. But we have little time to spare for these things now, as our all too short voyage is almost at an end and in a few minutes we shall be alongside.

As we run up to the Mole the Belgian flag is broken at the foremast head and men on the fo'castle are busy with the hawsers for making us fast; and now we are about to step ashore and begin another stage of our holiday, for surely the crossing has been a most enjoyable experience and in looking back we cannot but include the first twelve hours - and that is all the passage occupies - as being certainly not the least pleasant of our complete trip to the Continent.

Decorative Labels.

Cover of folio.

2) A New Humber Trader. The Queen of the Humber Fleet Arrives.
(**Hull News** 24 August 1925)

I have just had the privilege, through the courtesy of the Finland Line (Messrs John Good and Sons Limited, the local agents) of travelling from St. Nazaire, France, to Hull with the splendid new Finland liner **Oberon**.

Built by the Société Anonyme des Chantiers et Ateliers de St. Nazaire (Penhoet) she was handed over to her owners, the Finland Line (Finska Angfartygs Aktiebolaget) and sailed for Hull, arriving in the Victoria Dock early on Tuesday morning, in readiness to commence on the regular Hull-Finland passenger and cargo service for which she has been specially designed.

On arriving at the docks and shipyards of St. Nazaire, we had a little difficulty in picking out the **Oberon** as she lay alongside the fitting-out berth preparing for her departure, for although by no means the largest of the many vessels surrounding her, each in a different stage of construction, her white hull and finely-proportioned black funnel, with its familiar two white rings, made her conspicuous and in strong contrast to the grey and drab colouring of the unfinished vessels nearby.

Shortly afterwards tugs took us in hand fore and aft, the one remaining gangway was removed - after the usual last minute rush of people who wanted to be on or off the ship - and the 3,000 ton **Oberon** slowly began her journey towards the dock entrance.

Clear of the dock wall we were momentarily startled by the sudden deep bellowing blast of the syren (**sic**) as it spoke a parting salute together with the dipping of the Finska house flag and Finnish ensign to the builders.

At last we passed through the dock gates and out to sea between the two piers with their sentinel lighthouses and it was goodbye to St. Nazaire.

The **Oberon** is built to British Board of Trade Convention Rules, and Lloyd's highest class and to comply with French rules for passenger steamers. She has a length over all of 305ft 6ins and the whole of the upper deck from the bridge right aft is given over to the use of first class passengers and very pleasant it is too.

An inspection of the engine was suggested and down we went amongst the cranks, wheels and rods to the accompaniment of the ever thud-thud, thud-thud (surely music to an engineer) of **Oberon's** powerful 4,900 horsepower engines. These are of the reciprocating triple expansion type and at 102 revolutions per minute give a speed of 15 knots. One scarcely realises the power developed on watching such smooth running and perfectly constructed machinery and the vibration - so well are the grand cranks balanced - was during the whole trip almost imperceptible. This together with the great steadiness of the ship, was remarked by everyone. She is of course an oil burner.

The weather of Saturday being perfect for the purpose we wandered about the ship examining this or that appliance or chatting with the sociable Finnish officers under the command of Captain Sjolund, the late popular commander of the **Arcturus** who has been appointed to the new ship.

The 1st class smoke room, on the boat deck, provided a rendezvous for those who were tired of walking or sitting about in the open and desired a quiet smoke and chat. There are comfortable tub chairs upholstered in brown crocodile leather and the walls are panelled in walnut, the electric light and other fittings being in dulled silver. The windows are of a particularly novel design and the floor is done in black and white rubber tiling.

In the afternoon a carrier pigeon, much fatigued, and bearing messages, alighted on the bridge and caused a pleasant diversion. This uninvited extra passenger was given a warm welcome by the kindly officers and members of the party who vied with each other in enticing the bird with water and morsels of food. A further message was then added to those already carried - giving the ship's name, time, date etc and after a night's rest our winged visitor departed with the good wishes of all.

It had been suggested at dinner on Saturday that we should have a concert the following evening to celebrate **Oberon's** maiden trip and that each of us should contribute an item. Sunday evening came and we repaired to the music room, perhaps the most charming of the 1st class public apartments. It is carried out in a scheme of dark mahogany with costly chairs covered in grey velvet and a very novel frieze design (this latter also being a feature of the dining saloon). There is a piano and loudspeaker too. At nine o'clock the [break in the text] (Pour glorifier le Premier Voyage du bon bateau **Oberon**) - as advertised by a special poster overnight - began. A more jolly affair it would be difficult to imagine. We were fortunate in having, amongst the ladies, some first-class musicians, but some of the other 'artists' candidly admitted to having no accomplishments whatsoever. Anyhow, they simply made up for any shortcomings in that direction by entering wholeheartedly into the fun and their efforts were equally appreciated and applauded. Bearing in mind the different tongues spoken, it would be almost

impossible to give an adequate written description of the 'special items' rendered.

We wound up around midnight with speeches and toasts, expressive of the genuine comradeship which existed between the different people connected with the ship's designing and building and into whose care she is now handed.

Monday commenced for a few early birds with a visit to the bridge at six o' clock for a first sight of the English coast in the form of the white cliffs of South Foreland. The lightships marking the dreaded Goodwins gave us greeting with the bull like roar of their fog horns to which, as the day wore on we became more accustomed by the number of other lightships we passed.

By this time we had made a very complete inspection of the whole vessel with her accommodation for 132 first and 236 third class passengers, the conveniences and arrangements for the latter being of the highest order. We had also had pointed out the extra strengthening given to the hull of the vessel to withstand the strain of service amongst ice.

Twilight faded into darkness with the sea gently lapping our sides as we slowed down to pick up the pilot and our voyage was nearing its end. The powerful beam of Spurn Light seemed to welcome, in an appropriate way, the first arrival of the newest Humber trader and to guide her to what will be her journey's end on - we sincerely hope - many happy and prosperous voyages in the years to come.

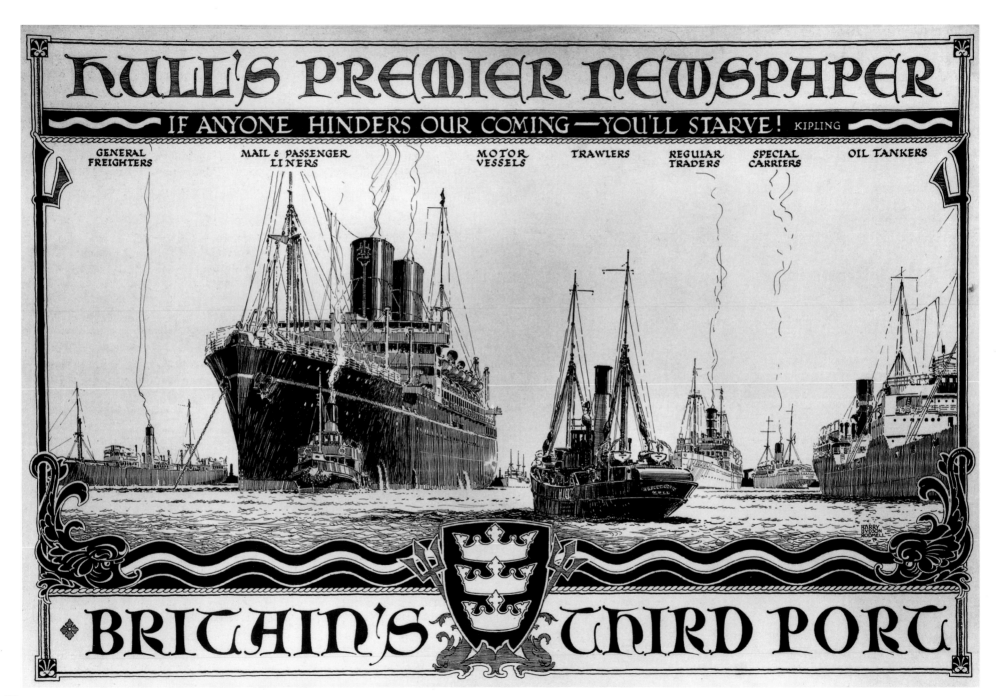

50

3) Modern Artists are not all Mad.
(**Hull Daily Mail** 8ᵗʰ September 1956)

'We take it for granted that music, medicine and other things must change.... in fact, everything except art' complained Mr. H.H. Rodmell when he spoke to Hull Rotarians on 'The Approach to Art'.

Complaining about the public's 'stick in the mud' attitude to art, he said 'Just as the engineer or doctor or scientist gives his life to further investigation, we must allow the artist, architect or sculptor to work with their own outlook.

Really Striving.
'New improvements in art are always sniggered at. But we must remember that the classics which we praised so much were in their time something new and were played down by the people of that time'. Modern artists were not all mad, he said. They were really striving and giving their whole lives to some other means of expression beyond the purely obvious. Their efforts should not be lightly dismissed. Mr Rodmell urged people to see good pictures and read about them. Just because a picture was beautifully painted and finished, and contained every possible detail, it was not necessarily good art.

Origimal pen drawing Hull's Premier Newspaper Britains Third Port, published 14th July 1926, Hull Daily Mail (17 ¹/4 in x 23 ¹/4 in).

4) Working in Line and Wash.
(**The Artist** Dec.1961 Vol. 62, No. 4, issue No. 370 pp74-76)

Drawing and draughtsmanship have fascinated me from early years and therefore it is perhaps not surprising that now I find line and wash to be one of my favourite means of pictorial expression. Line, in one form or another, usually provides the basis of most of my work either in watercolour or oils, and, although it may not appear evident at first glance, it is a fact that many of my pictures start as drawings made either with pen, pencil, chalk or brush. In the latter instance, the brush is used as point medium in order to commence with a vigorously drawn line.

In the first place it might be advisable to consider the varied and interesting materials available for our use. It never seems to occur to many of the amateur artists whom I meet at weekend painting schools and other gatherings that the orthodox pen and Indian ink is not the only means available by which we can produce the necessary line for our work. There are many different and exciting materials which we can use. Have you ever thought, for instance, of trying carbon pencil, quill or reed instead of a pen? There is also the aquarelle pencil which, when used on damp paper, gives a soft line of interesting quality. What about trying unfixed ink, coloured inks or watercolour with whatever 'pen' you use? It is surprising what varied effects can be achieved by being brave enough to dip a different sort of point into a different sort of ink! Paper, too, is equally important and worthy of experiment and until you have tried you can have no idea of the surprising and worthwhile results which can be obtained. What about tinted paper?

In a broad sense I think we may classify the use of line and wash under the following three headings: (a) Drawing the subject first and then adding the wash; (b) Applying the watercolour first and then drawing over it; (c) A combination of (a) and (b).

If you will refer to the sketch reproduced in colour; *Pyramid of Steel;* you will see an example of method (a). In this I followed one of my favourite practices, i.e. carbon pencil combined with watercolour. When employing carbon pencil for my line, I work with a 3B Conté or Wolff on as smooth a paper as will take a wash. The reason for this is that I like to work quickly with the point, and the feel of the pencil gliding over this sort of surface makes for a more vigorous handling than would be the case with a rougher surface. I find that Kent Hollingworth 'not' surface suits me very well and quite frequently I even use hot-pressed. I am well aware that the latter is not primarily intended for watercolour, but if the washes are laid on quickly with as broad a brush as possible the freshness will be preserved. When I am working in this medium, I commence with say, a half imperial sheet of stretched paper and sketch in, with the lightest touch, a few lines to indicate the position of the main masses; and from that point I go right ahead with the full strength drawing. I seldom trouble to fix the carbon but I am very careful not to drag colour over the heavier passages. A slight blending or smudging of some of the pencilling, if not overdone, can be very effective, provided it does not dull one's colour too much. *Pyramid of Steel* was done on the spot in about an hour and a half and left untouched.

The sketch of *Marton Woods* is an illustration of the second method. Here I worked in the reverse manner, also on the spot. The work was begun by floating masses of colour on to the paper without any preliminary drawing whatsoever. The paper was slightly damped and the areas of colour were very loosely applied to suggest the approximate positions, tones and colours of the trees, etc. The sketch was then allowed to dry completely, after which it was worked over with carbon pencil. It is most important that the paper should be absolutely dry before applying the pencil, otherwise an unpleasant, slimy line will be the result. This method makes for a rather looser handling because the colour is not so exactly bound by the outlines as when the drawing is done first.

St. Mary's, Beverley may be taken as an example of work under the third heading. This was drawn on hot pressed paper with a 3B carbon, again on the spot. In the first place the main lines were drawn in pencil in full strength and then the broad masses of light and dark colour were floated in, care being taken not to disturb the pencil too much, as it was not fixed. When the areas of colour had become quite dry, some detail was drawn in the pencil and a few further touches of colour added to complete the sketch.

Strictly speaking, *Holiday Harbour* does not come under any of the above three headings. Although it is a near monochrome and the method used is entirely different, it is nevertheless line and wash. It was drawn in the studio (from a pencil sketch made out of doors) on hot pressed paper in unfixed ink which was applied with a reed. Alternatively, I could have used a piece of thin cane cut slantwise with no nick and held with the cut uppermost. A fairly careful, though loose, and very light pencil drawing was made and the exciting job of rapidly inking-in began. Each section was more or less completed as the picture progressed.

When any part such as the funnel or hull of the ship called for solidarity, the near dry ink was touched with a not too wet brush; this caused the outline to run and form a wash. Other parts, such as the water, were just treated as ordinary wash using merely the diluted ink. Actually I added the faintest touch of yellow to the ink in places and this gave the original a slightly more interesting greenish-black effect.

When trying out new experimental techniques I find it easier to work in the studio. By so doing one can concentrate on the mechanics of the job and, if something interesting is the result it can be then tried out on the spot.

By the way, when working out of doors there is a tendency to see too much detail, especially if one is particularly interested in the subject for its own sake. When this happens the result can be laboured and fussy. Should this be the case, it is not a bad plan to use the sketch as a piece of information only and work it out again in the studio as a broader and bolder picture.

For those people who feel that their work is apt to become rather tight and lifeless, I think the following experiment may be found to be of some value. In the first place I would suggest that you choose an outdoor subject and then set yourself a time limit - say an hour - in which to make a complete sketch.

You must be absolutely firm in regard to this element of time and not fall prey to the obvious temptation of stealing the extra ten or fifteen minutes which you may feel necessary at the expiration of your time limit. Line and wash could be a very suitable method by which to carry out this time study.

Working with carbon pencil or pen and ink, you would have to attack the drawing at full speed and this would make for freedom of handling and vigorous strokes. Following this, the broad application of colour washes put in at full strength first time should result in a sketch which is full of life. You will find also that it is practically certain to have much more real quality than a work taking three times as long and with far more detail, but as dead as mutton!

Reverting to our main theme of line and wash, there is no reason why one should not use more than one sort of line on the same sketch. For instance, I have sometimes drawn with a carbon pencil and finally added detail with pen and ink. Again, I have used coloured aquarelle pencil for my soft original line and finished with touches of carbon, and so on. Mixing one's media if carried out with thought can effectively enrich the texture and quality of the work.

May I add one final and, in my opinion, particularly important piece of advice: whatever your medium or method of working do keep a sharp lookout for your tone values.

These suggestions by no means exhaust the possibilities of line and wash - indeed they are merely some of my own excursions into this fascinating technique. If, however, the reader has been encouraged to explore further on his own it may be that some useful purpose has been served and some exciting work will result.

5) Sketch From Memory
   (**Hull Daily Mail**, 6 March 1965)

Speaking to Hull Art Club last night Mr. H. Hudson Rodmell of Hornsea, one of the leading artists in the North-East said that one of the main faults of many workers was that they drew and painted too tightly.

They got bogged down with accuracy of detail and thereby lost the main impression of their scene or object.

To counter this, he advocated rapid drawing from memory, no rubbing-out, and the use of broad quick-moving utensils such as pens made from quills or reeds, charcoal or felt nibs.

Cartoon Drawing of Harry Rodmell in his studio: signed and dated 1924, Ern Shaw. Reproduced in the brochure **Exhibition of Ships and Humor**.

Cartoon of Harry Rodmell a float 'A ship-mate of mine'; signed Ern Shaw. Reproduced in the brochure **Exhibition of Ships and Humor**.

*Original pen drawing of S.S. **Jacobus**, Ohlson
Steamship Company, number 49, Humber Traders
series, 29th November, 1926, **Hull Daily Mail**.*

"EDINBURGH"

Original pen drawing at battleship H.M.S. **Edinburgh***; no. 11 in the Guardships of the Humber series, 11th October 1929,* **Hull Daily Mail***.*

Typical Poster site; Hull 1950s. (Harry Cartlidge).

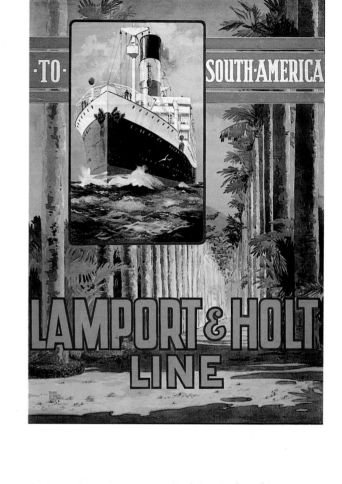

The s.s **Eskimo** built 1910 at Earles Shipyard, Hull for the Wilson Line; painted in poster colours. Recovered from the company headquarters, Commercial Road, it is not signed but is probably the picture Wilson's acquired from Rodmell c. 1914 (32 in x 42 in).

Birds-eye view of proposed new pier at Hull; entrance to Humber dock basin, left, and the river Hull, right. Signed and dated 1919 (watercolour; 26 in x 45 in).

Study for Lamport and Holt poster. Signed and dated 1919 (poster colour; 29 in x 20 1/2 in).

'All's Well'; silhouette of Statue of Liberty and four-funnel liner. Signed and dated 1919 (poster colour; 29 1/2 x 21 1/2 in).

Royal Holland Lloyd poster featuring s.s **Limburgia** launched 1914 as the **Johann Heinrich Burchard**, named **Limburgia** 1916-1922; renamed **Reliance** for United American in 1922. Signed and dated 1921 (Ronald Massey 23 Knightrider Street, London E.C.4).

Canadian Pacific; signed and dated 1921.

The s.s **Jupiter**, Bergen line; the small boat and timber posts were used in the Royal Holland Lloyd poster featuring the **Limburgia**. Signed and dated 1920 (watercolour; 20 ¹/₂ x 28 in).

The SS **Athenic**, Shaw Savill and Albion Line. A cargo passenger vessel built in 1901 for White Star to run joint service. In 1928 sold to become the whale factory ship **Pelagos**. Signed but not dated (watercolour; 17 ¹/₂ in x 23 in).

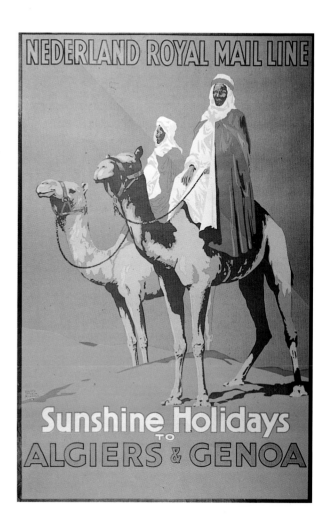

Netherland Royal Mail Line; not ships afloat but 'ships of the desert'! Signed but not dated (Ronald Massey 106 and 108 Victoria Street SW1).

*Finland Line (F.A.A); featuring the s.s **Oberon** which entered service in 1925 but was lost in collision with **Arcturus** in the Kattegat, en route to Hull. John Good and Sons Ltd, Hull, were agents for Finland Line. Signed but not dated. (Printed by Brumby and Clarke Ltd Hull and London).*

*Oceanic Steamship Company; featuring the **Ventura**, c. 1925. Signed but not dated.*

*William Watkins Ltd; tide tables for 1926; the tugs **Muria, Arcadia, Badia** and **Hibernia** shown towing the s.s **Rawalpindi** built in 1925 for the Peninsular and Oriental Steam Navigation Company. Signed (mounted on heavy card 20 in x 13 in).*

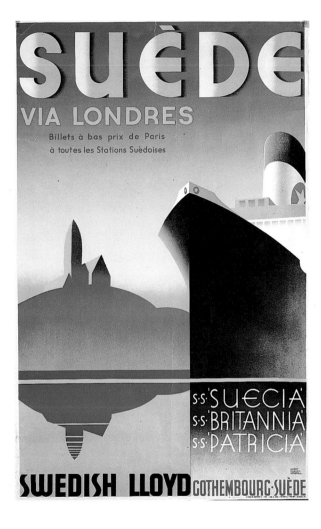

*Hamburg-Amerika Line; featuring the **Orinoco** built in 1928. Signed but not dated (Ronald Massey 106 and 108 Victoria Street SW1).*

*Swedish Lloyd; the **Patricia** (1926) **Suecia** (1929) and **Britannia** (1929) were all built by Swan Hunter on the Tyne. Signed but not dated (Ronald Massey 106 and 108 Victoria Street SW1).*

White Star Line calendar for 1929; signed (mounted on heavy card 14 1/4 in x 5 in).

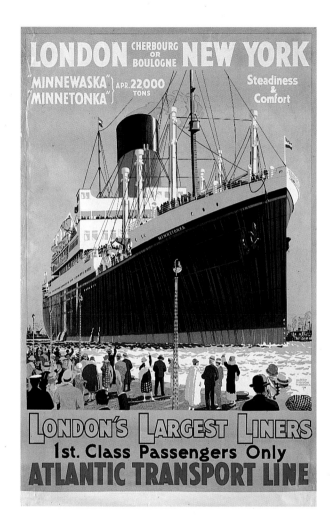

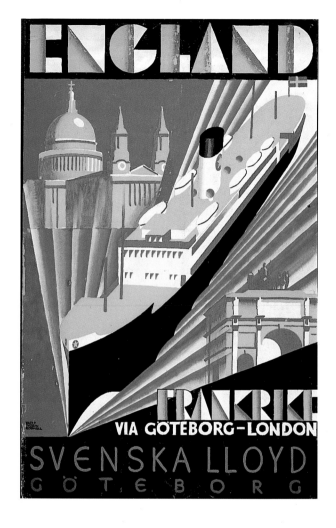

Atlantic Transport Line; featuring **Minnetonka** built in
1924 by Harland and Wolff of Belfast; **Minnewaska** was
launched in the same year. Signed but not dated (Ronald
Massey 106 and 108 Victoria Street. SW1).

Australian Commonwealth Line; signed but not dated
(Ronald Massey 106 and 108 Victoria Street, SW1).

Swedish Lloyd; study for a poster designed in the modern
idiom (30 in x 19 in).

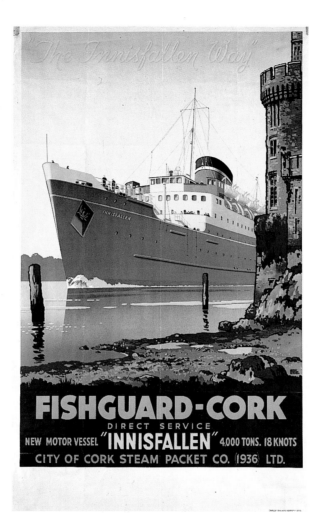

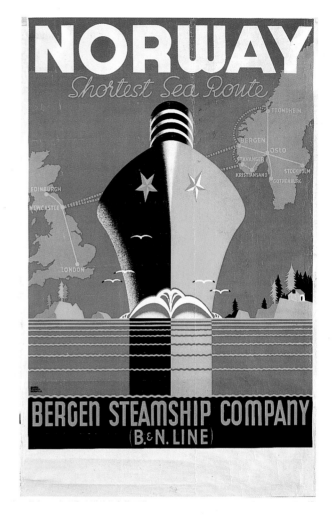

Trade of Hull and the Humber Ports; cover design for 1946. Signed (16 1/2 x 11 1/2 in).

*City of Cork Steam Packet Co; featuring the new **Innisfallen**, built 1948, by William Denny of Dumbarton (Carew Wilson Massey Ltd).*

Bergen Steamship Co; the identical design was used for the company's 1948 calendar. Signed but not dated.

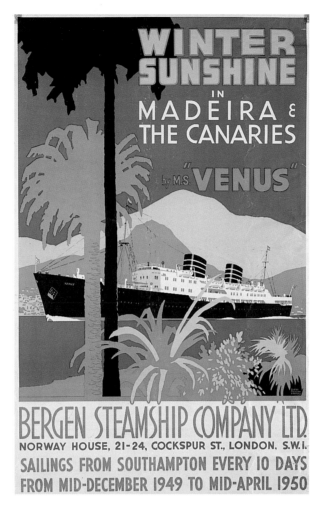

Burns Laird Line; signed but not dated c. 1950.

*Bergen Steamship Co Ltd, 1949-1950; featuring the M.V.
Venus built in 1932 but not scrapped until 1968. Signed
(Carew Wilson Massey Ltd).*

*Associated Humber Lines, 1952. Not signed (published
by Railway Executive, North Eastern Region, 1952 and
printed by Chorley and Pickersgill Ltd, Leeds).*

Bergen Line; featuring the M.V. Meteor built in 1955. Signed but not dated (Carew Wilson Massey Ltd).

Ship Towage (William Watkins Ltd, Gamecock Tugs Ltd and Elliott Steam Tug Co Ltd; tide tables for 1956. Tug Crested Cock towing a P and O liner. Not signed (18 in x 11 ½ in).

Burns and Laird. Not signed or dated (Carew Wilson Massey Ltd).

Associated Humber Lines; signed and dated 1959. (Published by British Railways, North Eastern Region, 59 and printed in Great Britain by Jordison and Co Ltd, London and Middlesbrough) (40 in x 50 in).

British Transport Docks Board; signed but not dated c. 1960 (printed in Great Britain by Jordison and Co Ltd, London and Middlesbrough).